A Journey
From Welfare to Yellowstone

A Journey
From Welfare to Yellowstone

Freed in the Wild

A Journey of Transformation

Laurie E. Spencer

A Journey from Welfare to Yellowstone

Freed in the Wild

Laurie E. Spencer

Dedications

First off, a huge shout-out to my amazing kids. Thanks for your endless patience and for jumping into the car every time I said, "Road trip!" without questioning it, even when you knew where we were going. Your trust in my sense of direction (or lack thereof) is truly commendable.

To my mom, who not only watched the kids but was also there for me as I traveled to the great unknown. You were the real expert on road trips.

And to my sisters, who supported me from both near and far. Even if you occasionally questioned my sanity (let's be honest, who would not?), your support means a lot to me.

Author's Note

This is a true story — mostly told from the driver's seat of life, with a few detours through memory lane.

Some names and identifying details have been changed to protect people's privacy (and, in a few cases, to protect the guilty). Certain events have been combined or slightly rearranged, so the story doesn't take as long to tell as it did to live. Conversations are reconstructed from memory — the kind that sticks with you when life gets loud, messy, and funny all at once.

Every emotion, every hard climb, and every laugh-out-loud moment is true to what I experienced. This book is my honest journey — from welfare lines to mountain trails, from brokenness to rebuilding, and from fear to faith.

So, buckle up—it's a bumpy road, but there are some beautiful views along the way.

Laurie E. Spencer

Table of Contents

Prologue

Years later, standing at the edge of Yellowstone's Grand Canyon wearing a ranger uniform I never thought I'd earn, I would remember the smell of that welfare office—institutional cleaning solution, stale coffee, and defeat. But on that Tuesday morning, clutching ticket number eighty-nine with three hungry kids beside me, I didn't know that Yellowstone was waiting. I didn't know that rock bottom would become a foundation.

I just knew we were out of milk.

I sat in a plastic chair that had been bolted to the floor—because apparently someone once thought stealing a chair from a welfare office was a good idea—and clutched Heidi's hand while Jason and Jacob fidgeted beside me. The fluorescent lights buzzed overhead, and every few minutes a woman's nasal voice crackled over the intercom: "Number seventy-three. Window four."

I looked down at the crumpled paper in my free hand.

Number eighty-nine.

Sixteen more people before it was my turn to prove I was desperate enough.

Heidi was six years old, her legs dangling from the chair, her wide eyes taking in the crowded room. Jason, eleven, sat with his arms crossed, trying to look tough. Jacob, ten, stared at the floor.

They'd eaten cereal for breakfast—dry, because we were out of milk.

"Mom?" Heidi whispered.

"Yeah, baby?"

"Why are all these people sad?"

I didn't have an answer that wouldn't break me, so I squeezed her hand instead.

Around us, the room hummed with quiet desperation. A woman bounced a crying baby. An elderly man coughed into a handkerchief. A teenager filled out paperwork with shaking hands.

We were all here for the same reason: we had run out of options.

I had spent years trying to avoid this moment. I had worked construction, built furniture from scrap wood, and stretched five dollars into three meals. But my marriage had ended, my truck had broken down, and the bills kept coming.

So here I was—a thirty-year-old single mother with three kids—asking the government to help me feed my family.

The voice crackled again. "Number seventy-four. Window four."

Fifteen more.

I closed my eyes and prayed: "God, if You're listening, show me the way out of this. Because I can't stay here. I won't."

I didn't know it yet, but that prayer would lead me from welfare lines to Yellowstone National Park. From homeless shelters to building my own cabin with my bare hands. From food stamps to freedom.

But first, I had to survive at number eighty-nine.

Introduction
A Choice That Changed Everything

A Choice That Changed Everything

This is not a story about perfection—trust me, you won't find any halos or harp music here. It's a story about perseverance, laughter, and a stubborn refusal to stay down, even when life threw curveballs, sinkholes, and the occasional bureaucratic avalanche.

When I packed my old Toyota pickup with everything I owned and left California, I wasn't chasing a dream—I was escaping a nightmare.

Picture it: one rusty truck, three kids, and a prayer that the tires would last longer than the money. I had no job waiting, no house, no five-year plan—just a campground reservation, a half tank of gas, and my mother's vague promise to meet us "somewhere along the way."

(This from a woman who had disappeared from my life for years at a time. But I'd worry about that later.)

At thirty years old, I already felt like I'd lived three lifetimes—and all of them came with overdue bills.

The first thing I asked my mother when she started sending letters from Colorado wasn't, "Can you help with childcare?" It wasn't, "Do you have room for us?" It wasn't even, "Why did you disappear?"

It was: "Are there spiders?"

Because California had spiders the size of small dogs, and I had priorities.

When she wrote back promising no big spiders, I thought, Good enough. We're going.

Look, I know that sounds ridiculous. Making a life-altering decision based on arachnid populations isn't exactly sound life-coaching advice. But when you're standing in welfare lines wondering if you'll ever escape… when you've been homeless with three kids… when every door seems locked—you grab whatever thread of hope appears.

Even if that thread is spider-free mountain air.

What you'll read in these pages is raw and real. There are moments of deep pain—childhood trauma, the sudden loss of my brother Steven to lightning, the humiliation of standing in welfare lines, and nights when I wasn't sure we'd make it to morning.

But there's also plenty of laughter, the kind that sneaks up on you when life is at its messiest. The kind that happens when your car sounds like a mobile percussion concert and you drive it to church anyway. The kind that emerges when you're building furniture from dumpster wood and calling it "vintage."

You'll meet mountain sunrises that made me believe in God all over again. Wild animals with better manners than some people. Tourists who asked when we "let the animals out." (The animals were not consulted on scheduling.)

And you'll discover that God has an outrageous sense of humor when you least expect it.

I grew up in a two-room schoolhouse in the San Bernardino Mountains, where the uphill walk to class was so steep it counted as my first gym membership. That's where I learned that life is mostly uphill—but the view is worth it.

Those lessons came in handy decades later when I found myself homeless with three kids, one truck, and enough faith to fill a thimble.

This journey took me from welfare offices in California to the rugged beauty of Yellowstone National Park, where I traded paperwork for pine trees and became a maintenance worker with more courage than experience. It wasn't a straight path—more like a scenic detour with surprise potholes. Along the way, I picked up life lessons from Utah farms, construction sites, and the occasional stubborn goat who thought he owned the place.

I discovered that sometimes progress looks like survival. And survival, blended with faith and humor, looks a lot like grace.

This book is for anyone who's ever felt stuck.

For single parents who wonder if life will ever calm down. For the tired, the broke, the overlooked, and the "how-did-I-end-up-here?" crowd. For anyone who's been told they're not educated enough, not skilled enough, not worthy enough—and started to believe it.

Here's the truth: your story isn't over.

Even when things seem bleak, overwhelming, or absurd (and trust me, they'll get absurd), your journey continues. I've stood in those same lines, faced that same fear, asked those same questions.

And yet, here I am—still standing, still laughing, still believing that faith can turn even the messiest story into something beautiful.

This isn't a fairy tale. There's no "happily ever after" with everything wrapped up in a bow. But there is transformation, the kind that happens quietly when you refuse to quit.

I carry scars from the road, yes, but I also carry proof that redemption is real, that laughter heals, and that God never wastes pain (though He sure takes His time sometimes).

In these pages, you'll meet my children:

Jason—my firstborn, the funny one who could make me laugh even when I wanted to cry. The one who moved out at nineteen by taking the TV while I was at work. The one I lost too soon.

Jacob—my middle son, who hated me for dragging him to Colorado and showed it by pretending to be asleep every time I came home. The one who eventually forgave me and became a master plumber.

Heidi—my fierce, independent daughter who got her first job at twelve and later beat cancer twice through sheer stubborn faith.

They were my constant companions, my comic relief, and the reason I kept going when quitting seemed easier.

You'll meet people who helped—angels in unexpected forms.

You'll meet some who hurt. And you'll meet others who disappeared faster than you can say "rent's due." You'll journey through mountains that healed me, jobs that humbled me, and faith that held me together like spiritual duct tape.

This story isn't about escaping poverty or finding success—it's about becoming whole. It's about discovering that even when the world tells you you're nothing, God whispers, "You're more than enough."

So whether you're standing at a crossroads or sitting in your own wilderness moment, I hope you find something here that makes you laugh, cry, and—most of all—believe again.

Welcome to the mountains.

Welcome to laughter.

Welcome to the journey from welfare to Yellowstone—and every messy, beautiful, impossible thing in between.

This is what happens when you refuse to stay down.

— Laurie E. Spencer

Chapter 1
Into the Unknown

The California border disappeared in my rearview mirror, and I felt something I hadn't felt in years.

Relief.

Not the kind you get from finding a parking spot or finishing your taxes. The bone-deep, soul-lifting kind that comes when you finally—finally—escape.

"Hotel California" was playing on the cassette deck. I jabbed the eject button and hurled the tape out the window.

"Mom!" Jason laughed from the passenger seat. "You can't just"

"Watch me," I said. "We're leaving. For real this time."

My old Toyota pickup groaned under the weight of everything we owned—clothes, camping gear, whatever else I'd managed to cram into our seventy-five-dollar utility trailer. The truck protested every mile, rattling and wheezing like it might give up any second. But we were moving.

Forward. Away. Out.

Heidi, ten years old and squeezed between Jason and me, pressed her small body against the stick shift. Every time I changed gears, she leaned with it, trying to give me room that didn't exist.

"How long till we get there?" she asked.

"Long enough," I said.

"But how long?"

"Baby, I don't know. A few days, maybe."

Jason—sixteen, lanky, and trying so hard to look like this didn't scare him—turned to stare out the window. We'd left Jacob behind at my sister Louanne's for the summer. One less body crammed in this cab, but one more piece of my heart somewhere else.

Jacob was my opposite son. Where Jason stuck close, Jacob pulled away. He was quiet, independent, always off with friends or at baseball practice. I made sure he never missed a game—even when gas money was tight, even when I was exhausted. Because baseball was his thing, and I wasn't going to take that from him.

But he made it clear: whatever I did, it wasn't good enough. In his mind, his dad, who barely called, who sent sporadic child support, and who'd moved on with his life—was somehow doing better than me.

It stung. But I kept showing up to those baseball games anyway.

The heat was already brutal, and it was only nine in the morning.

With no air conditioning, we rolled down the windows and let the desert wind blast our faces. Hot air whipped through the cab, tangling Heidi's hair and making my eyes water. Sweat trickled down my back, soaking into my shirt. The vinyl seats stuck to our legs.

Welcome to freedom, I thought. It's hot, cramped, and smells like an overheated engine.

But it was ours.

Behind us, in that rearview mirror, was everything I was running from:

The welfare office where I'd spent years proving I was desperate enough to deserve help.

The church community that had vanished the moment things got hard—where were all those people when we were homeless? When we needed a place to stay? When my kids' bikes got stolen and we couldn't afford new ones?

The family members who'd made comments about "their tax dollars" paying for my food stamps while simultaneously doing absolutely nothing to help.

The system designed to keep you dependent, punishing you every time you tried to earn a little extra money by cutting your benefits even further.

I was done. Done being stuck. Done asking for help that never came. Done with California.

"Are you okay, Mom?" Jason asked quietly.

I realized I was gripping the steering wheel so hard my knuckles had gone white.

"Yeah, bud. I'm great."

And I was. For the first time in years, I was no longer merely getting by—I was making my own choices. Choosing to leave. Choosing to take a chance. Choosing to believe that somewhere beyond this desert, there was a life worth living.

The cassette deck clicked empty, a little door swinging open like a mouth waiting to be fed.

"What else you got?" Jason asked, rummaging through the glove box. He pulled out three more tapes: a mix of country, oldies, and one labeled Church Songs in my friend's handwriting.

"Not the church one," I said.

He grinned and popped in the country tape.

Heidi wrinkled her nose. "I hate country."

"You'll learn to love it," Jason said. "Mom, we got any snacks?"

"There are crackers in the back."

"Just crackers?"

"And peanut butter. Maybe some apples, if they didn't roll under the seat."

He twisted around, trying to reach into the camper shell through the little pass-through window. His elbow jabbed Heidi in the shoulder.

"Ow! Mom, Jason hit me."

"I didn't hit you; I bumped you. There's a difference."

"It hurt!"

"Heidi, give him room. Jason, stop elbowing your sister. Can we make it ten miles before we start fighting?"

They both went quiet—for about thirty seconds.

We crossed into Arizona as the sun dipped toward the horizon, painting the desert in shades of orange and gold. The truck rattled on, held together by duct tape, prayer, and whatever miracle kept engines running when they should've died miles ago.

Heidi had fallen asleep against the door, her head pressed to the window. Jason hummed along to the tape, drumming his fingers on the dashboard.

"How much longer to Phoenix?" he asked.

I checked the map spread across my lap—one of those fold-out paper maps that never folded back the right way. "Maybe two more hours if we don't hit traffic."

"Think Grandma's plane landed yet?"

"Probably."

He was quiet for a moment. "You think she'll actually be there?"

That was the question, wasn't it?

My mother had a history of disappearing. Years would pass with no word, then suddenly she'd resurface like nothing had happened. Now she'd promised to fly from Denver to Phoenix, pick up a car for a friend, and help us drive to Colorado.

It sounded great on paper.

But I'd learned not to count on paper promises.

"She'll be there," I said, trying to sound more confident than I felt. "She said she would."

Jason nodded but didn't look convinced.

Smart kid.

By the time we rolled into Phoenix, the heat had gone from brutal to biblical.

It hit us the moment we stepped out of the truck at the airport—a wall of heat so thick you could practically see it shimmering off the pavement. It was late afternoon, and the temperature gauge on a bank sign read 112°F.

"It's like opening an oven," Heidi said, her face already flushed.

"Stay in the shade," I told her. "And drink water."

Jason scanned the crowd outside the terminal, looking for his grandmother. I was scanning too, trying not to think about what we'd do if she wasn't there.

We had enough gas money to get us to Colorado—barely. Enough food to last the drive if we were careful. And a two-week campground reservation waiting for us.

Two weeks.

That's how long I had to find a job, find housing, and figure out how to make this work.

After that? I had no idea. This had to work.

Please, God, let her be here.

"There!" Jason pointed.

And there she was—my mother, walking out of the terminal with a small suitcase, wearing sunglasses and looking exactly like someone who'd just flown in from cooler elevation.

She spotted us, waved, and headed over.

"You made it!"

"We made it," I agreed. "How was the flight?"

"Fine. Hot here, though." She fanned herself. "The car's at my friend's house. Not too far from here. We'll need to pick it up, then figure out where you want to caravan from."

Jason was already helping load her suitcase into the truck.

Which presented an immediate problem.

The truck was full.

When I say full, I mean Tetris-level, every-inch-accounted-for full. Three people already crammed in the front cab like sardines. The back was stuffed with everything we owned.

And now we needed to fit my mother in too.

"Uh, Mom," Jason said slowly, eyeing the truck. "Where's Grandma gonna sit?"

Good question.

I looked at the truck. Looked at my mother. Looked at my kids.

Heidi started giggling. "Should we tie Grandma to the roof?"

"Don't tempt me," Mom said dryly.

We did some creative reorganization. I climbed into the camper shell and shifted things around—moving boxes, redistributing weight, creating just enough space for Heidi to crawl back there through the pass-through window.

"You'll be okay back here?" I asked.

She nodded, already making herself a nest among the sleeping bags. "It's like camping!"

"We'll keep the window open so you get air from the cab," I promised.

Mom climbed into the front seat, grateful for the slightly cooler airflow. Jason took his usual spot by the passenger window. I squeezed behind the wheel and prayed this truck could handle the weight.

"All right," I said. "Let's go get that car."

I got us out of the area as quickly as I could and took us to my mom's friend's house.

By the time we finally had both vehicles and were ready to leave Phoenix, the sun had fully set, and the temperature had dropped to an almost reasonable ninety-five degrees.

Mom looked pale.

"You okay?" I asked.

"Just the heat," she said. "I'm used to mountain elevation. This desert air is killing me."

She wasn't exaggerating. She looked genuinely sick—face flushed, eyes tired, breathing shallow.

"You want to wait until morning?" I offered.

"No." She shook her head firmly. "Let's get out of this heat. The higher we go, the cooler it'll get."

Jason volunteered to drive the car she'd picked up—he was sixteen and had his license, plus he loved any excuse to drive something other than our ancient truck.

So we formed our little caravan: Jason leading in the newer car with Mom.

I followed in the groaning truck, with Heidi now stretched out in the front.

And finally—finally—we left Phoenix behind, heading north toward Flagstaff, toward higher elevation, toward cooler air.

Toward whatever was waiting for us in Colorado.

The highway climbed steadily, leaving the desert floor behind. The temperature dropped degree by degree, and I could see Mom starting to breathe easier.

Half asleep, Heidi murmured, "Mom? Are we almost there?"

"Not even close, baby," I said. "But we're getting closer."

In the rearview mirror, Phoenix faded behind us. Ahead, Jason's taillights glowed red in the darkness, leading us forward.

Two vehicles now instead of one. A grandmother who'd shown up when I'd half-expected her not to. Kids handling this crazy journey better than I had any right to expect.

Maybe—just maybe—this was going to work.

The road stretched ahead into darkness, climbing toward mountains I couldn't see yet but knew were waiting.

I pressed the gas pedal and kept following those taillights.

Behind us, Arizona. Ahead of us, Colorado.

And somewhere in between, the life we were going to build.

Chapter 2
Mountain Girl

I grew up in the San Bernardino Mountains, where I attended a two-room schoolhouse perched so high above Southern California it felt like the highway leading to it climbed straight into the sky. A mile and a half up a steep grade—one of those climbs that made your legs complain before you were even halfway there.

There was no kindergarten. You just jumped right in with the first-through-third graders squeezed into one room, while the fourth-through-sixth graders held court in the other. If your parents didn't drive—and mine rarely did—you had to walk. Rain, shine, snow, it didn't matter. You walked. Or, if you wanted a little thrill at the end of the day, you pushed your bicycle up the mountain so you could coast home.

And by "coast," I mean we dreamed about it while pushing those bikes like stubborn mules who refused to cooperate.

My best friend and I made that brutal 10% grade climb every single day. We had two short flat stretches on the route, and we treated them like we'd just reached heaven—tiny moments when our legs stopped burning long enough to remember what breathing felt like.

I packed lunches from whatever we had: bread that might've been fresh once, a smear of peanut butter if the jar wasn't empty, and a couple of snacks I scavenged from the cupboard.

But the ride home…

Oh, that was its own kind of magic.

Wind stung your face, pine trees whipped by in green blurs, and the whole world opened beneath your wheels. For those few minutes, you felt weightless, like you could lift right off the mountain and fly. The downhill freedom made every painful step of the morning climb worth it.

My sister Louanne and her friend rode sleek three-speed bikes—professional gear compared to our rattling clunkers. They treated the steep hill like a personal challenge, zigzagging back and forth like little engineers mapping switchbacks. Their goal? Make it all the way to the schoolhouse without touching a foot to the ground.

And one day, Louanne took things to a whole new level: she leaned over mid-pedal and took a sip from a water fountain without ever getting off her bike.

We stood there speechless.

It wasn't cheating. It was pure mountain-girl brilliance.

Watching her always made me think, Maybe I can do hard things too.

When the school bell rang, the mountain became our playground. We rushed to the swings, pumped our legs until our toes brushed the sky, and hung upside down on the metal bars like fearless little acrobats.

We played baseball in the dusty patch beside the school—half the bases were rocks we dragged into place—and no one ever minded.

After school, my best friend and I ran the trails until the sun slipped behind the peaks, inventing adventures that stretched through the trees. And on the days when the dirt path behind our houses felt just right, we'd race our bikes down them. Those rides felt like homemade roller coasters, the kind that made us laugh until our ribs ached.

Nature raised us as much as our parents did.

Winters were a world of their own. The big hill in front of our house became a snow-packed racetrack with a wicked turn at the bottom. Miss the turn and you'd end up in the brush—or worse. We climbed that hill over and over, breath puffing like steam engines, just to soar down it again.

One day, five-year-old Deanna announced she was ready for her first solo ride. With the confidence of Evel Knievel, she hopped on the sled, shrieked her way down the hill—and then completely forgot to turn. She shot straight over the embankment and landed perfectly perched on a drainpipe sticking out of the hill.

She sat there stiff as a statue until Sheryl and I reached her. We tried not to laugh too hard as we helped her down. Deanna didn't think it was funny at first, shooting us a five-year-old glare that said, "I could've died." But once she was safely on solid ground, she started giggling too.

Some mornings, my friend and I dragged old car inner tubes all the way to school. We'd hide them behind the schoolhouse and spend recess sliding down the hills like Olympians in training.

On snowy days, we would even slide home on the slick highway, since cars couldn't drive it anyway.

Walking home on winter afternoons was its own challenge. My fingers would go so numb I couldn't feel them. I'd tuck my hands under my armpits and pray I'd make it home before frostbite set in.

We didn't have fancy snow gear—plastic bread bags became our boot liners, and our winter wardrobes were jeans, sweatshirts, and whatever jackets we could scrounge up. Every now and then, Grandma gifted us with new coats or boots for Christmas, and that felt like striking gold.

Then came the monster storm.

It dumped several feet of snow overnight. The power went out for days. Roads disappeared. The whole world turned silent, white, and eerie. The school announced that if kids could walk there to pick up and drop off assignments, it would count as a school day. That's how desperate everyone was to avoid stretching the year into summer.

Mom—half-carrying two-year-old Deanna—walked with Sheryl, Louanne, my friend, and her mom. Snow swallowed our legs up to our knees. Fog wrapped around us like a cold, wet blanket. My eyelashes froze together. Every breath felt like swallowing ice.

When we reached the school, there was no warmth waiting. No electricity meant no heat, just a freezing classroom where we grabbed our homework and headed back into the storm.

At home, we worked at the kitchen table by the yellow glow of gas lanterns, our breath drifting in little clouds as we wrote.

The cold was miserable, but the soft flicker of lantern light made the moment feel strangely peaceful—like determination had its own glow.

Those winters taught me something I wouldn't understand until much later:

Even the hardest seasons hide pockets of beauty.

But mountain winters weren't the only challenges of my childhood.

Before we settled up high, Dad worked for the State Highways Division, and we hauled our single-wide trailer from one desert job site to the next. It felt like we lived in nine different deserts across San Bernardino County—each one hotter, drier, dustier. Every time Dad finished a project, we packed up our lives and moved again.

Eventually, Mom was done with the constant moving. She wanted roots, not wheels. My parents bought a 23-acre piece of land in Riverside County and called it "The Ranch." They dreamed of permanence.

But permanence, I learned, can disappear in a heartbeat.

A massive fire broke out not long after we arrived. Flames tore up the mountainside so fast we barely had time to grab the clothes on our backs. We left a half-eaten lunch—hot dogs on paper plates—still sitting on the table.

The fire scorched the ground right up to our front steps before firefighters stopped it. The house survived, but Mom's sense of safety didn't. When Dad got a good offer on the land, she didn't hesitate. We sold the ranch and moved again.

Not because it burned down—

but because it almost did.

Next came Forest Falls, tucked deep in the San Bernardino Mountains. It was supposed to be our permanent home. But Dad's highway jobs kept him gone for months at a time, and we still found ourselves bouncing from temporary housing near one work site to the next. We had an address, but we never felt settled.

Surviving the ranch fire taught me that nothing is guaranteed—not stability, not safety, not even your own home. Constant movement became the rhythm of our lives. That shift, that unpredictability, built a kind of rugged resilience in me—a toughness I didn't realize I'd need later, when I climbed into a rusty truck and drove across the country alone.

But even that resilience was about to be tested in ways no wildfire ever could.

Because after the mountains and the trailer parks and the near miss with the fire, the next place Dad's job took us was Needles, California.

The mountains shaped me in ways I didn't understand at the time. They toughened me, grounded me, and taught me how to survive constant change. I didn't know it then, but all that moving, all that starting over, all that learning to hold my balance on steep trails was preparing me for something harder than fire or snowstorms.

Life was about to lead us out of the mountains and straight into the desert—into a summer where the sky would open, lightning would fall, and everything I thought I knew about safety and childhood would shatter in an instant.

Chapter 3
The Breaking Point

One of those stops was Needles, California—a scorching desert town where an August thunderstorm would change everything.

I was five years old, almost six, ready to start first grade. We had been swimming in a cove next to the Colorado River near our trailer home when dark clouds rolled in. Thunder rumbled across the sky. My parents pulled us from the water, and we took shelter under the awning of a snack shack.

But Mom was worried the wooden awning might be hit by lightning.

"We need to get to the trailer," she said. "Now."

We ran.

My brother Steven was seven. Louanne was nine. Sheryl was eight. We bolted across the open field, racing the storm.

Then the sky split apart.

A deafening flash exploded overhead—three jagged branches of electricity.

One hit a sprinkler head, snapping it clean in two. Another struck the ground.

The third struck Steven.

He fell.

I screamed at him to get up. Dad scooped him into his arms and flagged down a passing car. After that, everything blurred—panic, headlights, and fear.

The next thing I remember is the hospital. Cold. Sterile. Silent.

We waited, clinging to hope.

It wasn't enough.

Steven was gone.

Insert from Louanne's Diary

A few days after Stevie's death, Sheryl, Laurie, and I sat on the living room floor, going through the things my brother had made in Vacation Bible School. He was so excited and talked about all the stories he learned that week, especially the stories about angels. We placed his little projects into a scrapbook to remember him.

I was nine years old, Sheryl eight, Stevie seven, and Laurie five. We attended a small community church in the mountains. Sometimes we stayed with our grandmother, who taught us the Lord's Prayer. Little did we know God was planting something in us that would carry us through what came next.

On the drive home to the mountains after his funeral, Dad drove in silence. Mom stared ahead like stone. My sisters slept beside me. I watched lightning flash in the distance, tears falling onto my hands. I whispered a prayer, asking God if Stevie was in Heaven.

The moment I started to pray, I felt a presence—warm, real, unmistakable. I knew Stevie was safe. I knew God was with us. And that night, I fell asleep with peace. No one will ever convince me it wasn't real.

Grief settled over our family like a heavy fog—thick, suffocating, inescapable. Grandma did her best to hold us together, but losing Steven overwhelmed all of us.

When fall came, I started first grade and tried to pretend life was normal, though nothing was.

Steven is in Heaven now, I told myself.

He's watching over me.

But none of it made sense. Nothing felt right. Everything reminded me of the storm.

School became unbearable.

In that tiny two-room schoolhouse, I sat in the back and stared out the window at the swaying pine trees. The teacher's voice was background noise. My mind drifted back to the thunder, the flash, Steven's small body falling to the ground.

No one asked if I was okay.

No one checked if I understood the lessons.

And when I fell behind—and I did—the teacher didn't help. Instead, she assigned me to the "Jolly Club."

Despite its cheerful name, it was punishment. Kids who hadn't finished their homework stayed after school for fifteen extra minutes while the "gifted" students—the ones she adored—went on special field trips down the mountain.

I spent a lot of afternoons in the Jolly Club.

It wasn't that I didn't want to do my homework. I simply didn't understand it, and I had no one to help. Dad worked long hours and was gone for weeks. Mom was drowning in her own grief. And the teacher was too busy with her favorites to notice kids like me.

So I fell further behind.

The message settled deep inside me:

You're not smart enough.

You're not good enough.

You're less.

That belief followed me for years.

But there was one bright spot.

Our next-door neighbor—a kind woman whose name I wish I remembered—invited my sisters and me to her house for lunch every day. No forced smiles. No awkward questions. Just warm food, a clean table, and steady kindness. Her kitchen smelled of fresh bread and soup. She fed us, made sure we were okay, and sent us back to school with full bellies and a sliver of comfort.

Those lunches were a lifeline.

Then, when I was eleven, crisis struck again.

Louanne, twelve at the time, was diagnosed with a serious heart condition. She needed open-heart surgery—risky, complicated, and terrifying. I didn't fully understand the odds, but I understood enough:

I could lose another sibling.

The surgery took place at St. Vincent's Hospital in Los Angeles, far from our mountain home. Dad juggled work with hospital trips. Mom stayed with Louanne while trying to take care of the rest of us.

I couldn't be there. All I could do was wait and pray.

The hours felt endless. Finally, word came: Louanne survived.

When we saw her, tubes surrounded her tiny frame. A breathing machine hummed beside her bed. Her chest was stitched from the base of her throat downward. But when she opened her eyes, she smiled—weakly, but real. She was still fighting.

Her recovery was slow and frightening.

But she did it.

Eventually, she healed, and life returned to something normal.

But the trauma remained.

Three years after Steven's death, the weight of everything finally crushed my parents.

They divorced.

The split was loud, bitter, and inevitable. Dad blamed Mom for running across the field that day. Mom blamed Dad for everything else. They couldn't be in the same room without screaming.

I was twelve when the divorce became final.

Already broken by loss, my world split again.

This isn't a story about how Steven's death defined my life.

It's a story about how, by age twelve, I learned that loss wasn't a single event but a constant state of being.

My safety nets—family, home, stability—were shredded.

I was emotionally alone, angry at the God who let it happen, and conditioned to believe I was one of the "less than."

The shame I carried was heavy long before I ever became a single mother.

That shame would follow me into the courtroom where my future would be decided. Where a judge would force me to choose which parent I wanted to live with---as if either option could fix what was already broke

Chapter 4
Finding My Place
(And Losing It Again)

The judge ruled that my two older sisters and I could choose which parent to live with—but first, we had to spend six months with Dad. My youngest sister, Deanna, would stay with Mom. At the time, Dad was living with Granddad and didn't have his own place. His girlfriend, Cecilia, offered her small one-bedroom apartment, so that's where we ended up.

At first, it didn't seem terrible. My sisters and I took turns sleeping on the bed and the floor. But it didn't take long to see the truth: nothing about this arrangement was going to be fair. Even though I was only two years younger than my sisters, I had an earlier bedtime and was excluded from their activities. Cecilia favored Louanne and Sheryl openly—and for reasons I still don't understand, she resented me.

One day, we went to Kmart. I paused to look at something, and when I turned around, they were gone. I searched every aisle before remembering the rule: go to the big clock at the front of the store. That was the meeting spot.

I stood there, watching the red second hand drag itself around the face of that giant clock.

Ten minutes.

Twenty.

Thirty.

Shoppers came and went, checking the time, adjusting their bags, but my family never appeared.

After an hour, fear settled into a sickening realization: they hadn't lost me.

They had left.

They had checked the meeting place, seen I wasn't there, and gone home anyway.

After an hour and a half, the fear hardened into quiet shame. I couldn't stand there any longer, looking like a forgotten item no one cared to claim.

So I walked home.

When I arrived, Cecilia's car was already in the driveway. Inside, my sisters were happily making cookies and ornaments, the house warm and full of laughter. Instead of concern, I was yelled at for not being where I was supposed to be. Dad sided with Cecilia. I was blamed for my own disappearance.

Weeks later, it happened again—this time at a crowded holiday mall. I lost sight of them, went to the parking lot, and found them loading the car, preparing to leave without me. I climbed in quietly, too numb to speak.

I was twelve, and those moments carved something deep inside me: insignificance. I wasn't wanted. I was tolerated.

When the six months were over, I made my choice. I moved back in with Mom—and for the first time in a long time, I could breathe.

Life became simple again. No favoritism. No being left behind. Just normal.

My grandmother lived in Colton, and every day after school she picked up Deanna and me. She fed us, steadied us, loved us with the kind of safety kids should be able to count on.

Meanwhile, Mom was earning her master's degree and attended night school. I'd ride my bike around campus while she was in class. I even joined a karate program that taught me discipline and confidence.

And the best part?

Summer.

Every year, the four of us—Mom, Grandma, Deanna, and me—camped for two weeks in national parks across the West. Yellowstone. Yosemite. The Grand Canyon. We hiked under enormous skies and sat around campfires telling stories. Those summers were magic. I felt like the world was bigger than the failures I carried.

Life stayed steady for three years.

And then everything shifted again.

At the start of my eleventh-grade year, my sister Sheryl moved back in with Mom. Overnight, Mom slipped into old patterns—favoring Sheryl, excluding me, criticizing everything I did.

The warmth we'd built disappeared. I went from belonging to being invisible.

I couldn't take it. I moved back in with Dad. Cecilia was gone, Louanne was in college, and at least I had my own room. Predictable neglect felt easier than sudden rejection.

I was attending Redlands High School then, a long commute from Colton, but I didn't mind the drive. What I minded was the school itself. The teachers didn't teach. We wasted time, learned nothing. After years of being overlooked, it felt like confirmation: education didn't matter—so neither did I.

Then I joined Police Explorers.

Everything changed.

The Explorers brought structure, purpose, and discipline. We wore uniforms, rode in patrol cars, and learned real police work. For the first time, I belonged to something. The officers respected us. They expected excellence—and acknowledged it when we gave it. No favoritism. No being forgotten.

I threw myself into it completely.

Around that time, Dad was still involved in motorcycle racing and wanted Louanne and me to race too. I tried. I even placed well in the California Grand Prix. But my heart wasn't in it. I'd spent years riding and racing, but it wasn't my passion. The disappointment on Dad's face didn't faze me—I had finally found something I loved, and it wasn't speeding through the desert.

By senior year, I'd had enough of Redlands High. I transferred to Colton High—and suddenly, learning felt possible.

The teachers cared. They taught with purpose. I wasn't just surviving in school anymore; I was thriving.

Then it happened: I made the honor roll.

I ran to Dad, beaming.

"Dad! I made the honor roll!"

He barely looked up.

"Huh. I got a letter about that a few weeks ago, but I figured they sent it to the wrong kid."

The punch landed hard. Even when I succeeded, he couldn't believe it. But I didn't let it stop me. I earned my diploma and walked across that stage with pride. I had fought for every step of that achievement.

After graduation, college felt impossible. Years of doubt had dug in deep. So I looked into the military—specifically the Navy. I toured bases, ships, and recruiting stations. It felt right.

I did well on every section of the entrance exam—except English.

The questions were full of grammar rules and sentence structures I had never been taught. My confidence collapsed.

I failed.

I studied hard and tried again. Failed. Tried a third time. Failed again.

The dream slipped away. It reinforced everything I feared about myself: that I was uneducated, inadequate, less-than.

While I was away on a summer trip with Mom, Grandma, and Deanna, Dad's new girlfriend gave away my Police Explorer jacket and hat to her brother—items I had earned and saved for. Another blow. Another reminder that I didn't matter in that house.

So I moved back in with Mom. By then, Sheryl had moved out.

I took a job with the forestry service—a youth program that didn't require a degree, just grit and hard work.

And that is where the next chapter begins.

Chapter 5
Choosing God Over Everything

I was eighteen when I met Ron.

I had just graduated high school and started working for the forestry service through a government youth program. The pay was small, but the work felt like freedom. After years of struggling in classrooms where I never quite fit, being outdoors felt like coming home. I came back each night smelling like sagebrush and dirt—exhausted, scraped up, and content in a way school had never given me.

Our crew of twelve spent long days cutting fire lines and clearing brush with axes, shovels, and Pulaskis. I was one of only two women across all the crews, which meant every day came with something to prove. The work was grueling, but I loved it.

One week, all four crew members came together for a joint project. During lunch, a guy from another crew sat beside me. His name was Ron. He was kind, soft-spoken, and funny in a way that made even the hardest workday feel lighter. We talked easily, and by the end of that week, he asked me out.

I said yes.

We fell in love the way young people do—quickly, completely, without stopping long enough to wonder what came next. He had a good heart, and at eighteen, that seemed like enough.

We married when I was nineteen. And for a time, life was good.

Jason came first, when I was barely old enough to understand what motherhood meant. Then Jacob. Then Heidi. Three babies in six years. Our house was suddenly loud, alive, and overflowing with toys, diapers, bottles, and chaos.

I loved my children fiercely, with every part of me. But the reality of raising three little ones while working construction was crushing. I came home bone-tired, covered in dust, my muscles burning—and stepped right into a second shift of crying babies, bills piling up, and a marriage straining under the weight of life.

The romance that began during quiet forestry lunch breaks was swallowed whole by sleepless nights, financial stress, and the relentless demands of parenting.

Ron and I stopped talking.

We stopped laughing.

We moved around each other like ghosts.

There were still good moments—moments worth remembering. Ron often worked two jobs to keep us afloat. On his days off, he'd drive the kids around at sunset when they were teething or sit in a tiny plastic kiddie pool while they splashed around him, his face bright with joy. He played with them for hours, made silly voices for bedtime stories, and filled our home with laughter during the early years.

Those memories mattered.

They still do.

But slowly, the cracks widened.

Ron started disappearing into the TV every night, lost in shows and sports while life happened around him. I was drowning in responsibility and loneliness while he drifted further from me—and further from God. His childhood wounds and painful religious upbringing had carved deep scars, and instead of healing, he simply let go. He lost sight of God altogether.

And in the middle of trying to keep us all afloat, I started slipping too.

By the time Heidi turned four, the loneliness had become unbearable. Not the loneliness of being alone—but the loneliness of sitting ten feet from someone who didn't see you anymore.

So, I went out with coworkers after work. Bars. Loud laughter. Too many drinks. A life that felt like an escape but was really just another trap. I told myself I wasn't doing anything wrong because I didn't bring alcohol home.

But I knew better.

I was searching for peace.

Comfort.

Connection.

What I really missed was God.

I didn't have the words for it then, but my soul knew. Something holy was missing.

Then one day, there was a knock on the door.

A woman stood on my porch, smiling with a warmth that felt almost impossible. She invited me to church.

It wasn't her words—it was the glow. The light in her eyes. I didn't know what I was missing until I saw it in her.

"Okay," I said. "I'll come."

That Sunday, everything changed.

The church was small but alive—full of real worship, real joy, and the unmistakable presence of God.

The sermon pierced straight through the numbness I had been carrying. Something in me cracked open. I could breathe again.

I gave my life to Christ that day. Fully. Completely. Without hesitation.

I quit smoking—a thirteen-year habit—cold turkey. I stopped drinking. I threw myself into church with everything I had. Every service. Every Bible study. Every prayer meeting.

I was starving for God.

And I was, finally, genuinely happy.

But Ron wasn't.

What began as irritation turned into resentment, then hostility. My faith shone a light on the choices he was making, and he hated what it revealed. When you're running from God, the last thing you want is to be married to someone running toward Him.

The fights started. Long, ugly battles that left me exhausted and shaken. He accused the church of manipulating me. He spied on services, made wild assumptions, and turned my faith into a threat.

One night, he said the words I knew were coming.

"You need to stop going."

"I'm not going to do that," I said quietly.

And that was the beginning of the end.

For six months, we fought.

Six months of spiritual warfare inside our home.

Six months of Ron demanding I choose.

Six months of tension so heavy it felt like walking on cracked glass.

Ron would argue just to argue. He criticized the church, the pastor, the members—anyone and anything connected to the peace I'd finally found. And every day, the pressure grew. The walls felt smaller. The air felt tighter. I felt like I was being squeezed from the inside out.

Then one night, everything came to a head.

He stood in the kitchen doorway, his face hard, his voice flat—cold, final.

"It's the church or me, Laurie. Choose."

The kitchen went silent. The refrigerator hummed. The clock on the wall ticked too loud. My own heartbeat thudded in my ears.

I thought about the kids asleep down the hall—Jason, ten. Jacob, eight. Heidi, barely four.

I thought about how I would survive. How I would raise three kids alone. How I would pay rent, keep the lights on, buy groceries. How terrified I was—raw, immediate, suffocating.

Then I thought about the woman who had knocked on my door six months earlier.

The light in her eyes.

The peace I'd felt the first time I walked into that church.

The way God had reached into the darkest parts of me and whispered, I've got you.

I thought about who I had been before—lost, drowning, pretending I was fine, going to bars, searching for anything to fill the emptiness, slowly dying inside a marriage that felt more like a tomb.

And I knew.

If I gave up God now, I'd lose myself completely. I'd go right back into that darkness. And this time, I wasn't sure I'd ever find my way out.

The words came from a place deeper than fear, deeper than logic, deeper than survival.

"I choose God."

Ron's face went stone-cold, like the words had stabbed him in the chest.

"Then we're done," he said.

"Ron—"

"I mean it, Laurie. We're done."

He walked past me, grabbed his jacket off the chair, and headed for the door.

"Where are you going?" My voice cracked, but I didn't move.

"I'm moving out."

"Ron, please. The kids—"

He paused with his hand on the doorknob. For a moment, I thought he might turn around. Might say something. Might give us one last chance.

But he didn't.

The door closed with a quiet click that sounded like the end of everything.

I stood in the kitchen alone, my Bible still sitting on the counter.

And then I cried.

Not because I regretted my answer, I didn't.

But I knew what it would cost.

I cried for a week. Fear, grief, and uncertainty crashing over me in waves.

How would I raise three kids alone?

How would we survive?

What had I just done?

But even through the tears, even through the terror, one truth held steady:

I had chosen God.

And no matter what came next—no matter how hard, how scary, how impossible—I knew I would not be walking back into the darkness alone.

I was relieved.

Hopeful.

But nothing changed.

The pattern repeated.

Fight.

Leave.

Return.

Repeat.

Finally, when I applied for food assistance and told him he had to sign for a separation, he looked at me dead in the eyes.

"No," he said. "I want a divorce."

And that was it.

Jason was ten. Jacob eight. Heidi four. I was alone. On welfare. Fighting to survive with three kids and a faith newly born inside me.

But even in all that loss, one truth stood unshaken:

I had found God again.

And no matter what came next, I knew—

I would not be walking into the darkness alone.

The hardest years of my life were still ahead.

But so were the miracles.

Chapter 6
Clanking Car

Heidi was six years old the first time I walked into the welfare office.

Six years old, still small enough to hold my hand tightly as we stood in line, her wide eyes taking in the crowded room, the tired faces, the heavy sense of defeat that hung in the air like stale cigarette smoke.

Jason was eleven.

Jacob was ten.

And I was a newly divorced mother with no job, no money, and no idea how we were going to survive.

Welfare wasn't a choice. It was the only option we had left.

When Ron and I separated, I needed food assistance—but to get it, he had to sign for a separation. Instead, he made himself clear:

"No separation. We're getting a divorce."

So that's what we did. One signature later, my marriage ended, and I was standing in a world I didn't know how to navigate.

The welfare office became familiar—the long waits, the paperwork, the questions designed to make you prove you were desperate enough to deserve help.

Every month, paper food stamps arrived in the mail. Actual stamps, not the EBT cards people use now. I rationed $200 to stretch through thirty days.

Our first apartment was tiny but functional. The problem? It sat exactly one mile from the elementary school. Too close for bus service. Too far for a six-year-old to walk alone.

So twice a day, every day, I walked Heidi to school and back. Four miles a day. Rain, heat, wind didn't matter.

Heidi tried to keep up, her little backpack bouncing as she marched beside me. Some days she complained, but most days she accepted it as normal. For us, it was.

She was my dress-up queen and my walking disaster—creative, fearless, and constantly bruised. She had a long-suffering cat named Cristina, who endured being dressed in doll clothes and pushed around the neighborhood in a stroller. That poor cat had the patience of Job.

"Heidi, that cat does NOT want to wear a bonnet," I'd say.

"She loves it, Mom," she insisted, while Cristina looked ready to file her own welfare claim.

Every week or two, I made the long bus trip to the grocery store with my food stamps. I bought what we could afford, hauled it home, and stretched every dollar like it was elastic.

The rest of the time, I stayed home—and built furniture.

Jason had appointed himself as my protector. He went everywhere with me, pushing the cart like a bodyguard… until we reached the feminine products aisle.

Then he evaporated.

"You done yet?" he'd yell from three aisles over.

"Almost," I'd reply, trying not to laugh.

The second I moved the cart away from that aisle, there he was again glued to my side.

When we moved into the apartment, we had nothing: no sofa, no table, not even dressers. So, I set up in the garage, using whatever scrap wood I could find. And somehow, God provided every piece.

If I needed 2x4s, there they were in the dumpster by the door factory.

If I needed paint, someone showed up giving it away.

If I needed carpet, a friend had access to office leftovers.

The biggest miracle? Two perfect sheets of 4x8 plywood sitting in a wash during a hike—like someone had put them there just for me.

Every time, I whispered, "Thank You."

It wasn't coincidence. It was God showing me that even when people failed me, He never did.

The furniture wasn't pretty, but it was functional—and it was ours. Every shelf and table was built from God's provision, piece by piece. I wasn't just building furniture. I was building faith.

When my truck ran, I'd pack lunches after church on Sundays and take the kids on picnics. Mountains, lakes, or just the park—it didn't matter.

Then my truck died. Completely.

Mom suggested I borrow Grandma's car since Grandma, now in her eighties, no longer drove. So, I visited Grandma, picked up her car, and headed down the driveway.

Then I looked in the rearview mirror—and there she was. This woman who could barely walk was suddenly sprinting after me, waving her arms.

She was convinced I was stealing her car.

I reassured her, promised I'd check in regularly, and eventually drove off.

Two weeks later, the flywheel went out.

If you've never heard a car with a bad flywheel, imagine the loudest clanking you've ever heard… then multiply it by ten. People could hear me coming from blocks away.

Clank. Clank. CLANK.

Other people have check engine lights. I had a full percussion section. The car didn't just clank—it performed. Every bump was a cymbal crash. Every turn added a tambourine shake.

I was driving a one-woman band toward poverty, and we were really nailing the crescendo.

The kids started rating the sounds.

"That one was a seven, Mom."

"No way—that was at least an eight."

We made it a game because the alternative was crying. And I'd already cried enough for one decade.

Still, every Sunday, we clanked our way to church.

One week, I picked up my friend and her four kids. She stared at me like I'd arrived driving a broken washing machine.

"What happened to the car?"

"Flywheel's out," I said.

Her expression said, "I need new friends."

Still—we made it to church.

Ron showed up, not to worship, but to give me a hard time, as usual.

"Not now, Ron," I said, and we clanked home.

The next week, a drunk driver rear-ended us. The car was totaled, but somehow still running. The frame twisted, the back doors jammed shut, and the car looked like it had been in a rodeo.

But did that stop me from going to church?

Nope.

Kids had to climb over the front seats just to get out, but we got there. Every arrival was a spectacle—clank, clank, clank—as if we were announcing ourselves with cymbals.

Ron tried to comment again.

"Not now, Ron."

Then Aunt Freda passed away.

My sisters and I were close to her, and I was determined to attend the funeral. The last thing I wanted was for Grandma to see the condition of her car, so I parked far up a hill and walked to the service.

Afterward, cars blocked the road for another funeral. The only way out was across the grass.

So off we went—clank, clank—across the cemetery lawn. Workers leaned on their shovels, laughing as we bounced our way out, mortified and giggling all at once.

We made one more clanking trip to church the following Sunday.

And yes, Ron was there again.

He opened his mouth.

"Not now, Ron."

And that was the end of old Bessie—the clanking car that somehow got us through one of the most chaotic summers of my life.

Soon after, a friend from church needed to sell her small car quickly. I bought it for a fair price, and suddenly we had transportation that didn't attract an audience. It wasn't fancy, but it ran. Quietly. Smoothly. Miraculously.

We finally had a car that worked, a roof over our heads, and a little breathing room.

But even with those blessings, survival still felt like treading water. Every step forward came with another setback. The welfare system—I called it "the vacuum"—was always there, pulling us back.

As the kids grew older, we found a small house closer to town. It wasn't much, but it was ours—a place where we could finally breathe.

The boys spent a lot of time at Ron's sister Rhonda's house. Rhonda and her husband, Hector, were wonderful to them. Their home became a haven—normal, steady, peaceful. I was grateful… even if it sometimes stung knowing my kids had a "normal" place that wasn't ours.

But the vacuum was still pulling.

And what I didn't realize then was just how deep it really went.

Chapter 7
The Vacuum

The decision wasn't made at some calm, well-planned moment.

It was born in a desperate, late-night reckoning with bills I couldn't pay, children I couldn't feed, and hope that had run completely dry.

The brutal truth hit me like a punch:

I had failed.

The strong mountain girl…

The police explorer…

The woman who worked herself to exhaustion…

None of that mattered.

I was standing on the doorstep of the state office, waiting for a handout, becoming another statistic.

Walking into the Department of Social Services for the first time felt like stepping into another dimension. The air was thick—not peaceful, but heavy—weighted down by a thousand silent stories of crisis. I sat in a hard plastic chair, gripping my leg and trying to breathe as childhood shame flickered through me like a phantom.

This was the place people ended up in when the world decided they weren't strong enough, smart enough, or good enough to do it on their own.

I kept my eyes on the floor, unable to look anyone in the face.

The old voice whispered with perfect clarity:

"You are not smart enough.

You cannot do this."

I was twelve again, sitting alone, forgotten, waiting by the clock.

Only this time, I wasn't waiting for my father—I was waiting for the state to confirm what my father and my teachers had taught me long ago: that I belonged to the "less than."

But rock bottom has a strange way of becoming a starting line.

Getting out of the trap was the true test.

People talk about welfare like it's a free ride, but they don't understand that in our neighborhood, almost everyone was on food stamps. It wasn't shame. It wasn't laziness. It was survival.

When I stood in the grocery checkout tearing paper food stamps from the booklet, nobody stared. Nobody judged. We were all in the same leaky boat, bailing water as fast as we could.

The worst part?

The part that ate at my soul?

I couldn't get out.

Every time I tried to get even a minimum-wage job, my food stamps were cut. The math never worked. If I earned a little money, the benefits dropped more than the paycheck increased.

The harder I tried to climb out, the harder the vacuum sucked me back in.

Then came the family voices, the ones who weren't there to help but were always there to judge:

"Our taxes are paying for your welfare."

As if I had chosen hunger.

As if I wanted this.

As if I hadn't worked myself raw trying to build something from nothing.

Funny thing—those same people never offered a place for my kids to sleep.

I was frustrated enough to scream. I wanted to work. I wanted to support my kids. I wanted to teach them that hard work mattered.

But the system punished me for trying.

So, what was the point?

Still, I tried.

Around that time, I made a decision that terrified me:

I was going back to school.

For years I believed college was for other people, the smart ones, the ones who didn't fall behind, the ones who weren't told they'd never make it. But then I learned about prerequisite classes. Work-at-your-own-level classes. Classes designed for people like me.

For the first time, college felt like it was possible.

I enrolled full-time at the community college.

Suddenly, my days became a marathon:

Drive the kids to three different schools, race to my own classes, then reverse the entire route in the afternoon. After homework, dinner, and laundry, I studied until my eyes burned.

It was exhausting.

But I felt something I hadn't felt in years:

Real hope.

Education, I believed, was my ticket out of the vacuum.

Then one afternoon, I walked out of class and stopped dead.

My car was gone.

Stolen.

I stared at the empty space, feeling that familiar sinking sensation. Naturally, I thought. This happens just as I gain momentum.

So, Heidi and I came up with a plan. We rode the bus to the mall and bought bicycles—cheap ones, just transportation with pedals. But they worked.

For three glorious weeks, those bikes were our lifeline.

Then someone stole my bike.

I stared at the empty rack and let out a laugh—the kind of laugh you use just to keep from falling apart.

"Of course," I muttered. "Why not?"

A few months later, I bought a motorcycle from my brother-in-law.

Looking back, I'm not sure I even had a proper license. But we had helmets, insurance, and desperation—and sometimes that's all you need.

The motorcycle became my everyday transportation.

Groceries.

School drop-offs.

Errands.

Church.

Everything balanced on two wheels.

Weekends were the hardest. With only one seat and three kids, we were stuck at home.

Finally, one Sunday, desperate for community, I created a plan that was more determination than logic:

Trip one: take Jacob to church.

Trip two: return for Heidi.

Trip three: go back again for Jason.

By the time I parked that bike for the third time, the kids were all there, and we were together—exhausted, windblown, but there.

After service, a kind soul offered all three kids a ride home.

A blessing if there ever was one.

I was comfortable on a dirt bike, but riding on pavement terrified me. I never went over forty-five. The freeway was a no-go.

Until that day I accidentally found myself on a freeway on-ramp with Jason on the back.

My heart pounded. My chest tightened. Cars flew by like missiles. Jason didn't say a word. I begged God for an exit.

Finally, one appeared, and I practically dove off it, shaking.

As soon as I bought a used car, I sold the motorcycle. I decided people like me had no business on one.

Eventually, the police called—they'd found my stolen car.

Abandoned.

Out of gas.

Emptied of all my belongings.

I paid the impound fees because even a hollowed-out car was better than none.

Small victories.

That's what I lived on—small victories and sheer stubbornness.

And then, finally, I caught a real break.

I got a job.

A good one. One that paid more than anything I'd ever earned.

For the first time in years, I could breathe.

My first paycheck came, and I paid all the bills, rent, utilities, everything. I felt proud again. I felt alive.

A week later, the phone rang.

The paycheck had bounced.

Every check I had written—rent, utilities, groceries—bounced with it. Late fees stacked like bricks. The landlord, patient at first, finally broke.

"I'm sorry," he said softly.

"But you'll have to leave."

Just like that—homeless.

The kids and I moved into Ron's house. Not because I wanted to, but because there was nowhere else.

The kids slept in his front room. I set up a small desk in the garage with one dim bulb and a cold concrete floor. That's where I did my homework late into the night—my breath visible in the frigid air.

Ron ignored us.

He slammed ice trays into the freezer.

Poured iced tea so loudly it woke the kids.

The father who used to splash with them in wading pools was gone.

I couldn't stay.

I scraped together what little money I had and bought a camping trailer. Tiny. No bathroom. No water. Barely big enough for the four of us. But at least it was ours.

Except… it really wasn't living.

It was camping in a closet.

Four people.

Zero bathroom.

And a lot of elbows.

We used the gas station at night.

We froze in winter.

We tripped over each other in the mornings.

Still—I kept going.

Three kids. Three schools. My own classes. The trailer. The exhaustion. The cold. The constant fight to keep moving.

Finally, the pressure broke me.

One morning, I loaded the kids into the car, took a deep breath, and drove them to the homeless shelter.

When you love your kids, you'll walk into fire for them.

And that's exactly what I did.

The vacuum had taken nearly everything—my hope, my dignity, my belief in myself.

But I wasn't finished.

Not yet.

But even as life steadied for a moment, I didn't know that another storm was already moving toward us—quiet, slow, and sure. The kind of storm you don't see until it breaks right over your head.

Looking back, I can trace the first faint rumblings, the small shifts I ignored, the warnings I brushed aside.

It's where the road bends again—sharper than I expected—and everything I thought I was ready for would be tested in ways I never imagined.

Chapter 8
The Shelter

Driving to the downtown shelter, a lump formed in my throat. The conditions were heartbreaking—overcrowded, unsafe, and riddled with drugs and despair. I understood that so many people needed shelter as desperately as we did, but I couldn't bring myself to expose my children to that environment.

I stopped the car, bowed my head, and prayed.

Lord, show me the way. Where do we go from here?

With renewed determination, I drove to the next town—one I knew was safer—and went straight to social services, hoping for a better option. There, I was directed to a homeless shelter that housed small groups in actual homes rather than large, crowded facilities.

Inland Temporary Homes in Loma Linda, California, opened its doors in 1991, offering a different kind of shelter for families experiencing homelessness. Unlike traditional shelters, they placed families in residential-style housing, fostering a sense of normalcy and stability. By 1994, they were beginning to offer longer stays and more comprehensive services. But when we arrived, it was still primarily a place to sleep, with limited support or services.

Walking through those doors for the first time was overwhelming.

We received free basic toiletries—brushes, toothpaste, soap. It was a small gesture, but at that moment, it meant everything. After all the chaos we had left behind, the safety and cleanliness of the shelter felt like a blessing from God. It was a place where my children could finally sleep without fear.

But while the shelter provided a roof over our heads, it also came with strict rules that felt suffocating. Life there was governed by an unforgiving schedule. Each family had a designated time for cooking, eating, and cleaning, and if you weren't finished on time, you were rushed out so the next family could take their turn. Interaction between families was forbidden, as if relationships might disrupt the strict order.

Leaving something as simple as a coffee cup in the dish drain instead of immediately drying it and putting it away brought sharp scolding. Once we checked in by 5 p.m., the doors were locked behind us. No stepping outside for fresh air. No evening walks to clear my head. The world outside the shelter seemed so close, yet so far away.

Everyone, including the kids, had assigned chores inspected with military precision. The smallest infraction—like missing a spot while sweeping—brought correction without mercy. Privacy was nonexistent; we lived side by side with other families, each of us trying to hold on to whatever dignity we had left.

It didn't feel like a place for healing; it felt like walking a tightrope, always one misstep away from losing everything again.

Mornings began early. I would drop Jason, fourteen, at his bus stop first, with Heidi, nine, and Jacob, thirteen, tagging along groggy and cranky because I couldn't leave them alone. We weren't allowed to stay behind at the shelter during the day, so our mornings had no choice but to start early. Often, Heidi and Jacob would curl up half-asleep in the truck while we waited for their own schools to open.

From there, my schedule was relentless. I attended college classes during the day, pushing forward toward a better future. Since we couldn't return to the shelter until evening, afternoons were often spent in parks—my children playing nearby while I tried to focus on my textbooks, fighting fatigue and worry at the same time.

Evenings added their own layer of challenges. Attending my one-night class required special permission from the shelter, and even then, I couldn't leave the kids alone. I had to drive them back to their dad's house before class, adding extra stress to an already packed day. There was no such thing as spontaneity. Every move had to be pre-approved, accounted for, and explained.

One night, desperate for a sliver of normalcy, we left the shelter as usual for my night class—except I skipped class so I could visit a friend I hadn't seen in weeks. I just needed to talk to someone who knew me outside of these circumstances, someone who saw me as more than just another homeless mother struggling to survive. We returned to the shelter at our normal time.

That night reminded me that I was still me. I still had dreams, hopes, and a life waiting to be rebuilt.

Residing in the shelter fundamentally transformed my life. At first, the rigid structure felt like a prison.

But within that structure, something unexpected happened: I began to rebuild. The rules forced me to slow down, reflect, and confront the broken parts of my life. Some days I felt trapped. Other days, I realized that the same restrictions kept me steady, giving me enough stability to take the next step forward. The shelter wasn't just a place of restriction; it was a place of transformation. It stripped away the noise, the distractions, and even my excuses, forcing me to face my own resilience.

I learned discipline.

I learned patience.

I learned perseverance.

And most of all, I learned that sometimes the hardest places we find ourselves in are the very places that push us toward the life we were meant to build.

There were nights I lay awake long after lights-out, staring at the ceiling, wondering if this was what "starting over" really meant. I prayed for patience, for strength, and sometimes just for one quiet night where I did not have to fight so hard to keep it together. Yet in that discipline, something unexpected began to form, a quiet endurance. God was teaching me how to survive structure before I could appreciate freedom.

But I was learning these lessons alone.

When we needed support most, our church disappeared. The pastor left—packed up and moved to another congregation.

Without his leadership, the church fell apart. The congregation split. The tight-knit community I'd poured my life into, where I'd taught Sunday school and led Bible studies, simply dissolved.

My friends knew.

My family knew.

My church knew.

And they did nothing.

Nobody offered us a place to stay.

Nobody helped with groceries or gas money.

Nobody checked in to see if we were okay.

We were homeless. And nobody cared.

Or maybe they cared enough to feel good about themselves—but not enough to help.

Meanwhile, family members who had judged me for being on welfare still made comments.

"Our taxes are paying for your welfare," they reminded me, even as I stood there—literally homeless, with nowhere to go.

I wanted to send them a thank-you card:

Dear Family, thanks for the $0.37 of your annual taxes that fed my kids this month. Your generosity is overwhelming.

But I didn't.

I kept moving forward, one exhausting day at a time.

As our time at the shelter came to an end, I knew we needed a fresh start. The high unemployment rate in California made it hard to envision a stable future, even with a degree in hand. I began to dream of leaving the state, of starting over somewhere new. I shared my plans with my ex-husband, uncertain of how it would all unfold but determined to move forward.

Just in time—before we had to commit to another month at the shelter—I found a modest house to rent. It was an older house, and I knew I could fix it up.

And it was ours.

That lesson carried me into the next season of our lives—one marked by new roads, unfamiliar places, and the steady unfolding of God's plan beyond the walls of that shelter. And though the past still lingered, I felt the first glimmer of hope that this time, we might finally be moving toward something lasting.

Just when I thought we might finally have a roof that didn't leak, a floor that didn't squeak, and neighbors who didn't stare like we were aliens, I realized starting over was less about fixing a house… and more about surviving the next chapter of life.

Spoiler alert: it was going to be a doozy.

Chapter 9
Our New Home

Jason and Jacob were in high school by then, while Heidi was still in grade school. As we settled into our new home, the kids adjusted to their new schools, and we did our best to make ends meet. Each month, we scraped by on welfare and state assistance, with barely anything left after rent. After paying for utilities, there was only enough money to get to school and back.

Entertainment was a luxury we couldn't afford, so we kept it simple. Weeknights were for homework, and weekends meant scouring the house for four quarters to rent a movie for our old VCR. If we were lucky, we found enough to watch two. The rest of our free time was spent hiking in the nearby woods, a simple joy that never lost its magic.

We were still struggling, but we had a home.

And in that home, hope started to take root again.

We started hiking with my sister Louanne and her family. Despite everything we were going through—the shelter, the constant stress—we'd pile into the Toyota pickup I bought from a friend after selling the car, and we would head into the nearby mountains.

Those hikes were our escape. A chance to breathe fresh air, see something beautiful, and pretend, for a few hours, that life was normal.

One weekend, we planned a hike, and I needed to pack lunch for my kids. Tuna sandwiches and brownies were our go-to. But I ran into a problem: no baggies. No plastic containers either. I had to be creative.

"Aluminum foil," I decided.

I laid the sandwiches and brownies on a baking sheet, covered everything with foil, and shoved it into my backpack. Problem solved. Sort of.

That day's hike was no joke—steep, rocky inclines for over a mile, followed by another two miles of rugged trails. The kids, carrying the water bottles, raced ahead. I, on the other hand, was lugging a backpack that may or may not have looked suspiciously bulky.

When lunchtime rolled around, Louanne pulled out her usual spread—perfectly packed sandwiches, individually wrapped snacks, and neatly sealed drinks. Meanwhile, I reached into my backpack and pulled out… an entire nine-by-thirteen baking pan wrapped in foil.

Louanne took one look and burst out laughing.

"Are you serious?"

"I didn't have baggies," I said sheepishly. "So… I brought the whole pan."

She thought it was the funniest thing she'd ever seen.

There I was, lugging a pan of brownies up a mountain like it was some kind of prized treasure.

The kids didn't care. They tore into the brownies with sticky fingers, chocolate smearing across their faces as they devoured every bite.

To this day, Louanne still laughs about my "brownie trek."

On another hiking trip, as we were driving to the trailhead, a weird, lingering smell started creeping through the truck. It wouldn't go away, no matter how much I rolled down the windows. It wasn't the fresh pine of the woods or the earthy scent of nature… no, it was unmistakably skunk.

"Did we pass one on the road?" I wondered aloud.

But as we pulled up to the trailhead, the smell was still there stronger than ever. Louanne and Randy, with their noses as confused as mine, thought the same thing: maybe we'd accidentally hit a skunk.

But as we all stood there, sniffing the air like a group of confused bloodhounds, we realized the smell wasn't leaving. In fact, it was following us.

Jason popped the hood of my truck, and—surprise! —there was the little culprit, curled up in the engine like he was on a cross-country road trip.

Somehow, this skunk had hitched a ride all the way to the trailhead without a care in the world. We left the hood open, hoping he'd take the hint and make his getaway.

After the hike, we came back to the truck, and guess what?

The skunk was gone, but the smell was still there—like an unwanted guest who just wouldn't leave. My kids refused to get back into the truck. They all raced to jump into Randy's car.

Louanne, being the brave soul she was, hopped in with me, and we set off for home with our noses held high and our windows rolled down.

Randy, following us behind, eventually passed us by and refused to even follow us home. The smell was so overpowering, it was like a skunk-themed car chase.

When we finally got home, I had to leave the truck hood open for days to let the smell dissipate.

Those hiking trips, ridiculous as they were, reminded me that even in the darkest times, there was still joy to be found. Still laughter. Still moments of absurdity that made life bearable.

But underneath it all, the weight was building.

Then, a few months later, every single one of the kids' bikes disappeared from our property. All of them. Gone.

I stood there, staring at the empty space where the bikes had been, and something cracked inside me. Take my car. Take my bike. But do not take my kids' bikes.

This wasn't about the bikes—it was about everything. The years of trying and failing. The jobs that didn't work out. The paychecks that bounced. The car that got stolen. My bike that was stolen. The kids' bikes that were stolen. The system that trapped me. The people who judged me but never helped.

I was done.

Done with trying to fix everything on my own. Done with pretending I could carry it all. Done with believing that faith meant never breaking.

In that moment, standing in the silence where laughter used to be, I finally let myself feel it all—the anger, the loss, the exhaustion.

And in that breaking, something shifted. I didn't know what came next, but I knew this: God would have to meet me here, because I had nothing left to give.

I couldn't stay in California anymore.

The vacuum had swallowed everything—my hope, my dignity, my sense of possibility. This place had become a trap, and I was suffocating. The system kept me poor. The people who claimed to care never showed up. I was fighting a battle I could never win.

I didn't know where we'd go. I didn't know how we'd get there. But I knew, with absolute certainty, that we couldn't stay.

And that's when I remembered the postcards.

My mom had been writing to me from Colorado—specifically from Estes Park, a place she'd fallen in love with after moving there. Her letters were full of descriptions: the mountains, the fresh air, the sense of possibility.

She'd paint pictures with her words about life in a small mountain town, so different from the concrete and chaos of Southern California.

I'd read those letters during the hardest moments, letting myself imagine what it might be like to start over somewhere new.

Somewhere the air was clean and the mountains were tall. Somewhere that wasn't this endless trap.

Maybe—just maybe—Colorado was the answer.

The pull I'd felt as a child during those summer camping trips with my mom and grandmother—the pull toward mountains and open spaces—came rushing back. Those trips had planted something in me: a love for the wild, for the kind of freedom you can only find far from the noise of everyday life.

I felt that pull again now. A whisper that said, Go.

Somewhere, the air was clean, the mountains were tall, and the only thing I hoped would get stolen this time was maybe a pinecone—not my sanity.

Colorado was calling.

And this time, I was ready to answer.

Chapter 10
Hope in the Mail

It was December, right before Christmas, when the first letter arrived.

Heidi was about nine years old. We were settled in our house, and for a brief moment, life seemed steady. But underneath it all, that familiar restlessness still gnawed at me—the feeling that California would never let me go, that I'd be stuck in that same exhausting cycle forever.

Then I opened the mailbox and saw the envelope.

Mom's handwriting. A return address from Estes Park, Colorado.

I stood there for a long minute, just staring at it. Mom—who had drifted in and out of our lives since Heidi was two, who vanished for months or years at a time after remarrying—was writing to me.

Part of me wanted to toss the letter straight into the trash. After everything, why should I care?

But I opened it anyway.

Her letter was simple. Hi, how are you? How are the kids? Little updates about her job and life, nothing deep, nothing emotional. But there was something in her tone I hadn't heard in years. A steadiness. A calm. A softness.

She sounded… different.

Like she was trying to be apologetic without knowing how.

And honestly? I was happy to hear from her. Despite everything, she was still my mom. And if she'd finally found some kind of peace, some kind of stability—maybe that meant something.

Over the next few weeks, more letters came. And with them, postcards.

Beautiful postcards of Estes Park—clean streets with charming shops, snow-capped mountains glowing in the sun, elk wandering through open meadows like they owned the place. It looked unreal. Peaceful. Safe.

Her letters talked about riding a trolley into town, her job, the scenery, little stories from her days. Nothing dramatic. Just… life.

I started writing back. Cautiously at first. I asked about the weather, the cost of living, what it was like working at the YMCA.

And then, in one letter, I asked the most important question of all:

"Are there spiders?"

Not Can we stay with you? Not Why did you leave?

No. Spiders.

Because California's spiders were huge, and I hated them. And because asking about bugs was easier than asking about abandonment. Easier than digging up the mess between us. Easier than admitting I was desperate enough to consider moving across state lines to live near a mother who felt like a stranger.

Her response arrived a week later:

No spiders, she promised.

And the letters kept coming—more frequently now. She sounded genuinely happy, and that happiness seeped into me. Slowly at first. A tiny whisper.

Hope.

It grew with every envelope I opened.

By February, I couldn't ignore it anymore.

I wrote:

"When I have spring break in April, maybe I could come visit? My friends are driving through Denver on their way to Kansas. I could catch a ride."

Her response came fast. She knew I didn't have money, so she offered to pay for my flight home.

That unconditional offer—that olive branch—broke something open in me. For years, my mother represented abandonment. But being a single mom on welfare was its own kind of threat. I was exhausted. I needed help, even if it came from a shaky source.

So I gave myself permission to accept it.

I decided to fly there—not just to visit, but to see if this new version of her was real. To see if there was a future for my kids in a town I'd only seen on postcards.

For the first time in years, I had something to look forward to.

April finally arrived, and I climbed into a U-Haul with my friend who was moving to Kansas. She didn't want to drive alone, so I offered to come along. We drove straight through to Denver, where her husband waited. Then we made the winding drive into the mountains.

And then we arrived in Estes Park.

The air hit me first, crisp, clean, cool. Nothing like the smog-choked heat I'd been breathing for years. I took a long breath and felt something I hadn't felt in a long time.

Peace.

The town was tucked into a valley surrounded by towering mountains. Charming shops lined the streets. Tourists strolled through town like stress didn't exist. Elk grazed wherever they pleased. Everything was clean. Beautiful. Safe.

It felt like stepping into another world.

Mom arranged two complimentary rooms at the YMCA, where she worked. My friends stayed in one, and I stayed in the other. For a couple of days, we explored everything—Rocky Mountain National Park, the trails, the views. Everything felt magical.

When my friends left, I stayed behind.

That's when I truly began to see Estes Park.

Every morning, Mom went to work, and I explored. I hiked quiet forest trails. I wandered into small shops. I talked to locals. Everywhere I went, the community felt warm and welcoming.

And I started looking for work.

In California, getting a job felt like winning the lottery—hundreds of applicants for one position.

But here? The first place I applied—a machine shop—offered me a job on the spot.

I couldn't take it, not yet. I had to finish the school year, get the kids, tie up loose ends. But still—a job after one application? That was a sign.

I spent time at the YMCA too, watching families laugh and kids play. It was everything I wanted for my children. I thought about applying there but hesitated. Mom worked there, and I'd always had to be independent. Still, something about the place felt like home.

By the fourth day, I knew.

I was sitting on a bench downtown, staring up at the mountains, when the certainty washed over me:

This is where we're supposed to be.

Not a question. Not a maybe. A knowing. Peace stitching itself into my bones.

That evening, I told Mom.

"I'm coming back," I said. "Not just to visit. We're moving here."

She didn't even blink.

"I thought you might," she said, smiling.

A few days later, I said goodbye—not with sadness, but with direction.

I was returning to California with a plan.

I wasn't going back to stay.

I was going back to pack my life and leave it behind for good.

Little did I know that trading California chaos for mountain peace wouldn't be as simple as packing a few boxes. Moving across states with kids, no money, and a hope built on postcards?

Let's just say—Colorado had surprises waiting for me.

And not all of them came with pretty mountain views.

Chapter 11
Leaving

The flight home felt surreal. I stared out the window as the mountains disappeared beneath the clouds, my mind spinning with questions. How would I pack everything? Where would we live? What about the kids' schools?

But beneath all the logistics, something steadier stirred, a quiet conviction that this was the right move.

Excitement.

For the first time in years, I wasn't just surviving. I was moving toward something. Something better. Something real.

When I landed in California, everything felt different. The smog, the noise, the heaviness of the place—it pressed down on me harder than ever, now that I knew freedom existed somewhere else.

I couldn't wait to tell the kids.

Jason lit up the moment I said we were moving to Colorado.

He wanted to get out of California as much as I did. He'd carried the weight of our struggles too, and the idea of a fresh start filled him with the same hope I'd felt in those mountains.

Heidi, now ten, was nervous but excited. Leaving her school and friends was scary, but she trusted me.

When I described the mountains, the YMCA, and the trails we could hike together, her eyes brightened.

"Okay, Mom," she said softly. "Let's do it."

Jacob, however, was not on board.

He loved his school, his friends, and the sense of belonging he'd finally found. After everything we'd been through, Jacob was the one who had made a life here. He had good teachers, close friends—a rare stability that none of us had enjoyed in years.

He threw a fit.

We argued.

We talked.

Finally, we reached a compromise: Jacob would stay with my sister Louanne for the summer, finish out his time with his friends, and fly out to join us in the fall.

It wasn't perfect, but it was the only way forward.

With the kids mostly convinced, I turned my attention to the monumental task of packing.

Packing the Past

School ended in May, and June became a whirlwind. One afternoon, driving through town, I spotted a small utility trailer for sale. Seventy-five dollars. Affordable—but completely out of reach at that moment.

My heart sank. There was no way we'd fit everything into just the truck. I needed that trailer.

A week later, paycheck in hand, I drove back, expecting it to be gone.

But there it was—still sitting in the same dusty spot, like it had been waiting for me.

I thanked God for the tiny miracle and bought it on the spot.

Back at home, I grabbed a roll of tape and measured out the exact dimensions of the truck bed and trailer floor. Then—right there in my tiny front room—I taped out the outline and started stacking everything we'd take.

If it fit inside the taped-off box, it came with us.

If not, it went into storage.

Ron's family had an empty garage, and despite the tension between us, they agreed to let me store our belongings there—though not without comments.

"Colorado has fifty-foot snowdrifts!" Ron warned.

"You're making a huge mistake," someone else said. "You'll be back in six months."

This from people who never lifted a finger when we were homeless.

I didn't care anymore. Their opinions didn't fit in the taped-off rectangle, so they stayed behind too.

The Longest Month of My Life

The hardest part of June wasn't packing—it was the waiting.

I knew where we were going. I knew it was right.

But I still had to sit in California, in that spider-infested house (which was ironic, considering my first question to Mom had been about spiders), counting down the days.

It felt like being trapped in a cage with the door unlocked but someone blocking the exit.

Every night, I lay awake thinking of Estes Park—fresh air, mountains, hope.

Every morning, I woke up thinking, One day closer.

Finally, July arrived.

My last welfare check came on July 1st—the timing couldn't have been more perfect. That money, meant for a month of survival in California, would now be stretched across state lines until I could find work in Colorado.

The Fourth of July weekend.

Independence Day.

Honestly… you couldn't script it better.

I loaded the last of our belongings, adjusting tie-downs for the fifteenth time. Jason climbed into the passenger seat, Heidi squeezed into the middle, and Jacob stood with Louanne, waving as we pulled away.

We drove past the welfare office.

Past the shelter.

Past the church that had fallen apart.

Past every place that had nearly broken me.

And for the first time in years, I felt it:

Freedom.

The road stretched ahead, leading toward mountains, fresh air, and possibilities I could barely imagine. My old Toyota groaned under the weight of everything we owned, but it was moving forward.

We were moving forward.

And for the first time in forever, I wasn't running away from something.

I was running toward it.

Of course, I had no idea that the real adventure wouldn't start on the mountain roads—it would start about three hours into the drive, when my overloaded truck decided to test my faith, my patience, and every tie-down strap I owned.

Chapter 12
Onward

The California border disappeared in my rearview mirror, and I felt my chest loosen, my breath come easier. We were free.

"Hotel California" played on the cassette deck one last time. I skipped ahead, hoping to find something that matched how I felt—because I had checked out. I was leaving.

Jason sat by the passenger window, Heidi squeezed in the middle with the stick shift pressing against her leg. The truck groaned under the weight of everything we owned, the little utility trailer rattling faithfully behind us. With no air conditioning, we rolled the windows down—hot desert air blasting our faces—but I didn't care.

For the first time in months, I wasn't rushing to get somewhere on time. There was no welfare appointment, no shelter curfew to beat, no three-school drop-off schedule dictating my morning.

We had one destination: a campground. Somewhere. Anywhere. Wherever we felt like stopping.

It was the most liberating feeling I'd ever experienced.

By late afternoon, our first stop was Phoenix International Airport, where Mom had flown in from Denver to pick up a car for a friend.

The plan was simple: she'd get the car, Jason would help drive it, and we'd caravan together to Colorado—two vehicles, safer that way, and company for the long road ahead.

The moment we stepped out of the truck at the airport, the Phoenix heat hit like a physical wall. It was oppressive, suffocating—the kind of heat that makes you wonder if you've walked into an oven.

When Mom stepped off the plane, I realized calling our truck "full" was an understatement. It was a clown car: Heidi and Jason crammed into the front like sardines, the back looking like a Tetris game gone horribly wrong—piled high with everything we owned.

Jacob had stayed behind at Louanne's for the summer, which meant one less body to squeeze in, though I carried the weight of missing him and worrying about whether he'd ever forgive me for this move.

What I hadn't planned for was how we'd fit Mom into the truck.

There was barely room for the three of us in the front seat. I half-joked that I should have tied a rocking chair to the roof and let her ride up there like we were the Beverly Hillbillies.

In the heat, I scrambled like a circus performer, trying to clear a path through the mountain of clothes and supplies in the camper shell—enough space for Heidi to crawl back there. We opened the pass-through window between the cab and the camper so she could get cool air from the front.

It wasn't glamorous, but somehow, we got Mom into the truck. Barely.

With our load somewhat reorganized, we made a swift escape from Phoenix—though navigating the sprawling city was no easy feat. First, we had to cross town to pick up the car Mom had come to retrieve. With Jason now old enough to drive, he took the wheel of the second car. Heidi eagerly reclaimed her front-seat spot, and Mom, grateful for the air conditioning in her vehicle, settled in for the ride.

Just when we thought we'd found our rhythm, the Arizona heat took its toll. The drastic shift from her usual high-altitude coolness to the blistering desert air proved too much for Mom. She fell ill, adding another challenge to our already chaotic journey.

Still, like any good road trip, we pressed on—determined to reach our destination.

By the time we left Phoenix, Mom was clearly sick.

"Are you okay?" I asked.

"I'll be fine," she said—but I could see she wasn't.

"We need to get out of this heat," I said, studying the paper map spread across my lap.

Paper maps—that's all we had. No GPS. No smartphones. No electronic voice calmly redirecting us when we took a wrong turn. Just folds, creases, and our best guesses about which roads would take us where we needed to go.

We decided to head toward Flagstaff, where the elevation would bring cooler temperatures and relief from the relentless sun. The drive felt endless, but when we finally arrived and found a campground, the mountain air was like a gift. That first deep breath of cool, pine-scented air made the entire journey worth it.

That night, surrounded by towering pines, we set up camp. The kids helped pitch the tent while Mom rested, still recovering from the brutal Phoenix heat. As the sun set and the temperature dropped, we cooked a simple meal over the fire and talked about the road ahead.

"How are you feeling?" I asked Mom.

"Better," she said—and this time, I believed her.

We sat together—mother and daughter, two women who'd been through their own separate struggles—and planned our route through the mountains. We'd take the scenic byways, winding through cooler elevations, avoiding the interstates and the heat. It would take longer, but we had time. For once in my life, we had all the time in the world.

No deadlines. No appointments. Just the open road and the freedom to take it at our own pace.

The next morning, we set out again with a renewed sense of adventure. The scenery shifted from desert to forest, from flat expanses to towering peaks. Each turn brought a new sight—a canyon, meadow, or stunning mountain view.

We stopped frequently. Mom still needed breaks to recover, and honestly, so did we. The truck groaned under the weight of our belongings, the trailer swayed on sharp curves, and the lack of air conditioning made every mile feel longer than it was. But there was something beautiful about it, too.

The slow pace gave us time to notice things: the way sunlight filtered through the trees, the wildflowers dotting the hillsides, the quiet moments when it was just us and the open road.

No traffic, no noise, only the hum of the engine and the wind through the windows.

We camped every night, sometimes at established campgrounds, sometimes in clearings we found along the way. Heidi and Jason helped set up the tent and gather firewood.

Mom, stronger each day, told stories about Estes Park and the life waiting for us there.

There was no pressure. No schedule. If we were tired, we stopped. If we saw something beautiful, we pulled over. If we wanted to linger at a campground for an extra morning, we did.

This wasn't just transportation.

This was healing.

For years, my life ran on a schedule tighter than a church potluck line. Be here, go there, hurry up, keep moving. Every minute choreographed, like I was living to the rhythm of someone else's stopwatch.

But out here? Out here, I was in control.

We moved when we wanted. We stopped when we were tired. We explored when curiosity struck. It was freedom in its purest form.

Four nights. Four different campsites. Four opportunities to sit around a fire, stare up at the stars, and remember what it felt like to just be.

By the time we crossed into Colorado, I felt something shift inside me. This wasn't a road trip. This was a journey from mere survival to new opportunities.

The landscape changed as we climbed higher into the Rockies. The air grew crisper.

The mountains rose around us like ancient guardians, their snowcapped peaks piercing the sky. Everything felt bigger here—the sky, the trees, the sense of space and freedom.

And then, finally, we saw the sign: Welcome to Estes Park.

I pulled over for a moment to take it in. The town stretched out before us, nestled in a valley surrounded by mountains. Charming shops lined the streets. Elk grazed in open meadows. Everything looked exactly like the postcards Mom had sent—except better, because now I was here, and this was real.

"We made it," I whispered.

Jason grinned. Heidi pressed her face against the window, wide-eyed. Mom pulled up beside us, rolled down her window, and smiled.

"Welcome home," she said.

But we didn't have a home yet, not really. What we had was a reservation at a campground in Rocky Mountain National Park, where we'd stay for two weeks while I looked for work and housing.

The park was breathtaking—towering pines, clear streams, and wildlife wandering freely through the campsites. We set up our tent in a spot surrounded by trees, and for the first time in months—maybe years—I felt like I could breathe.

Mom's tiny employee-housing room was cozy but barely big enough for one person, let alone an entire family.

It wasn't the fresh start I had envisioned. The weight of it hit me some nights when I lay awake, wondering if this was the right path. But I reminded myself: this was temporary. We had already made plans for the next campground, and for now, that was enough.

We knew the journey wasn't over. In many ways, it was just beginning.

Rocky Mountain National Park became our next home for two weeks. We found a small storage unit for our extra clothes and supplies, which was a relief—less stuff to shuffle around, though there was still plenty of chaos.

I threw myself into job hunting, spending hours at the phone booth with my friend, trying to project bravery while my stomach churned with nerves. There was no turning back; only forward, toward whatever lay ahead.

As the days passed, I settled into a rhythm—days filled with work, nights spent in campgrounds, moving from one to the next. The uncertainty remained, but so did our resilience. We were like nomads, moving between temporary havens, trying to create a sense of home from nothing more than our togetherness.

Estes Park became both a haven and a reminder of how much we had to prove to ourselves. With each campground imposing a fourteen-day limit, our lives were in constant motion—finding the next spot, adapting to the next unknown.

I managed to secure a job at Safeway. Not glamorous, but steady. It gave me a sense of purpose.

That night, after the kids settled into their sleeping bags, Mom headed back to her small employee room at the YMCA. The YMCA provided housing for single employees—enough space for a single bed, a dresser, and a few small appliances, with shared bathrooms down the hall and meals in the main dining hall.

I stood outside our tent under the stars.

The stars were brighter here—clearer, more abundant than I'd ever seen.

I thought about everything we'd left behind: the welfare office, the broken system, the people who'd judged me but never helped. The stolen car, the stolen bikes, the endless disappointments.

And then I thought about everything ahead—the job I hoped to find, the home we'd eventually get, the life we were going to create here in this beautiful place, far from everything that had kept us trapped.

The road had been long. Uncertain. Exhausting.

But we'd made it.

And this was just the beginning.

We'd made it to Colorado with nothing but a trailer full of chaos, a truck that wheezed like an asthmatic donkey, and hope held together with duct tape.

But little did I know… the next chapter in my life wasn't about survival.

It was about discovering the true villain of mountain life:

tourist season.

Chapter 13
Building a Life in the Wild

We arrived in Estes Park in early July with everything we owned packed into a truck and a tiny utility trailer. No house waiting. No clear plan beyond "find a campground and figure it out from there."

Rocky Mountain National Park became our first home—a beautiful campground surrounded by towering pines, deer wandering through at dawn, and the sound of streams trickling nearby. It felt like paradise compared to California. But there was a catch: we could only stay for two weeks. And the cost? It felt like paying rent back in California—except our "apartment" was a patch of dirt and a picnic table.

Every campground in the area had the same rule—fourteen days maximum, then you had to move on. The few that didn't have time limits cost nearly as much as rent. We couldn't afford to stay anywhere long.

Within the first two weeks, I walked into Safeway, applied for a job, and was hired almost immediately. Finally, a steady income.

But even with a paycheck coming in, we were still camping, still packing up every fourteen days, still stretching every dollar as far as it would go.

My days fell into a rhythm: wake up at the campsite, get the kids ready, and drive them to the YMCA.

The YMCA became their second home, where they could play, skate, and be kids while I worked. Thanks to Mom's employment there, the kids' activities were free, a blessing I didn't take for granted.

Mom looked after them like a superwoman, making sure they were safe and happy while I clocked in at Safeway. Sometimes, in rare moments, we'd sneak into the employee shower rooms at the YMCA. The warm water felt like a luxury, a small escape from the chaos of our days. Even in those tiny moments, we found peace.

After my shift, I'd pick up the kids, and we'd head back to whichever campground we were staying at that week. We'd cook dinner over the fire, tell stories, and fall asleep to the sound of wind rustling through the trees. When my workdays stretched late into the night, Mom became our rock. She'd sit with the kids at camp, often falling asleep in a thrift-store lounge chair while waiting for me to return.

She never complained, despite needing to wake up early for work the next day. And neither did I. There was no time for complaints—only survival, only resilience.

Over those first nine weeks, we moved through five different campgrounds.

Each move meant packing up, finding a new spot, setting up again. By the fifth move, we had it down to a science—but that didn't make it any less exhausting.

Eventually, we found a spot on the free forest land, a deserted area far from town—quiet and isolated.

It wasn't ideal, but it was free. After weeks of draining our limited funds on campground fees, free felt like a gift. Those nine weeks of camping were some of the most exhausting—and strangely beautiful—of my life.

One night, a violent thunderstorm rolled through our campsite. We huddled in the truck as lightning turned the cab into a spectacle of flashing lights. Every strike lit us up like X-ray skeletons—all bones and wide eyes. The kids thought it was hilarious, and honestly, so did I. We stood there as thunder echoed and lights flickered around us like an animated scene.

But beneath the laughter came a sudden, haunting memory—of Steven. Of that August day when lightning took him from us. Of the terror and helplessness, I felt watching my brother fall. This time, though, we were safe. The storm battered outside, but we were safe together in the truck. And as I sat there, watching the lightning illuminate the mountains, I realized something: we'd survived more than just this storm.

As the weather grew colder, the crowds disappeared, leaving just us—me and the kids—spending frigid nights alone.

Each night, the wind howled like a wild animal, and I bundled the kids close, wondering how much longer we could endure this nomadic life.

Six weeks in, finding permanent housing in Estes Park still seemed impossible. The thought of returning to California crossed my mind, but I refused to go back to that system's suffocating grip.

That life was no longer an option. Kansas became our fallback—a temporary refuge with friends where we could regroup and try again next year. I was determined to move forward, to break free from mere survival.

That night, as another storm approached, I pulled out my journal and wrote:

In the Wilderness of the Rockies

I huddled beneath the covers of my sleeping bag, seeking refuge from the howling wind that seeped through the seams of our family tent. The night sky was ablaze with lightning, illuminating the mountains in stark, ephemeral brilliance, while thunder rumbled like wild beasts unleashed. Trembling, I drew the covers tightly around me and offered a fervent prayer. I implored for divine protection—strength to endure the cold, the isolation of the forest, and the uncertainty of finding a new home for my children. I prayed for a chance to begin anew, to rekindle hope and forge a fresh start.

"Ah, California," I murmured, longing for the spirit that once propelled me forward in that sunlit land, now seeming so distant.

My thoughts meandered back to my old home, the familiar mountains, the comforting ocean, the warmth of old friendships, and the security of family.

Once, during my school days, I dared to dream. A dream of liberation, of stepping boldly into the unknown. I yearned for freedom from the shackles of fear and failure, a stable job, a nurturing environment for my children, and the realization of my goals.

I envisioned buying a car, settling old debts, and residing in a charming abode. My dream was to embark on an adventure into new territories, to conquer fears and doubts, and emerge renewed.

Could I really leave everything behind and succeed? Was it possible to cleanse my past and start anew? Could I learn to believe in myself, escape the clutches of poverty, and discover a more promising environment?

These questions stormed through my mind, each one a tumultuous wave of anxiety and hope. Burdened by defeat and heartache, I packed my belongings and departed with unwavering resolve, refusing to look back.

It was "Colorado or Bust"—our destination a mere dot on a map, a campsite number waiting for us. Driven by a blend of desperation, faith, hope, and the thrill of the unknown, we embarked on this quest. The initial weeks were thrilling—exploring unfamiliar lands, meeting fresh faces, and even securing a new job. Yet soon we faced relentless winds, piercing cold, and blinding lightning. My endurance was tested to its limits. I began to doubt whether I could continue, questioning the sacrifices I had made for my children.

Despite my weariness and the temptation to abandon our journey, I found myself too exhausted to return home, too proud to admit defeat.

The voices of old friends faded into memory, and the allure of my mission seemed like a distant dream. I resolved to try again another summer, another year.

Though the winds of discouragement and fear battered the campfire, the embers glowed with hidden warmth. As I gazed one last time at the flickering flames, I pondered, Is there a greater challenge than stirring the spirit amid defeat? The urge to persevere began to overpower the temptation to quit.

Blowing gently on the coals, I discerned the comforting voice of the Lord urging me forward: "Go on, I will be with you."

Summoning every ounce of strength, I rose, bowed my head in prayer, and took a decisive step toward our future. Many weeks had elapsed since we left California—weeks of living beneath the stars, exposed to the elements.

No shelter to shield us from the rain, no walls to buffer the wind, and no coverings to ward off the cold. Amidst this wilderness, we hoped and prayed for divine provision.

Then, a vision unfolded before me. I found myself in a celestial room, where Jesus sat upon His throne.

I approached Him, fell at His feet, and He commanded, "Rise, take My hand!" I grasped His hand, and together we walked down a path leading to our new home, a rewarding job, and a secure environment for my children. Jesus assured me that He would provide for all our needs.

When morning came, I knew what I had to do. I couldn't give up. Not yet. Not when God had shown me the path forward.

Another storm rolled through one night, turning our truck into a spectacle of flashing light and sound. Lightning cast eerie shadows across our faces, making us look like cartoon characters caught in a flashbulb nightmare. As the storm raged, I couldn't help but reflect on our journey.

After weeks of searching, we finally found an affordable, cozy two-bedroom house with beautiful wood floors—a symbol of hope. But the waiting game continued.

Another week stretched on before we could move in. The challenge of supporting three kids felt overwhelming, and the arrival of Jacob only added to the emotional weight.

Desperate, I reached out to friends in Kansas, arranging for Heidi to stay with them until we had a home. Watching her board the plane, I felt both relief and fear—relief that she'd be safe, fear of what lay ahead.

That night, we camped at Garden of the Gods National Monument—homeless but hopeful. As I stood at the airport, fear washed over me. How would I bring Heidi back?

Would we ever be reunited?

Jason and I walked around Colorado Springs, uncertain about what lay ahead.

When Jacob arrived at the airport that same day from California, he took Heidi's place in the back of the truck.

The days of bitter cold continued, but we were nearing the finish line. The day before our move, I spotted a discarded mattress and box spring by a dumpster. My body ached from sleeping in the truck, and the thought of lying on a hardwood floor seemed unbearable. I hesitated, but the boys read my thoughts and loaded them onto the truck.

The next day, I drove to work with the mattress tied down, the promise of our new home pushing me forward.

Moving in was a lesson in minimalism. We had only our camping supplies, thrift-store finds, and our clothes. With the boys starting school and Heidi still away, the house felt empty.

Then, a call from a friend changed everything—she offered to pay for Heidi's flight home.

And just like that, our family was whole again.

We'd survived California. We'd survived the system that tried to keep us trapped. We'd survived homelessness, doubt, and every person who said we wouldn't make it.

And we were still there. Still moving forward.

By September, after nine weeks of moving from campground to campground, we finally found a place to call home.

It was a small, two-bedroom cabin with beautiful wood floors. Nothing fancy, but it was ours. A roof over our heads. Four walls. A door we could lock.

The problem? We had almost nothing to put inside it.

When we moved in, all we had were our camping supplies—a tent we wouldn't need anymore, sleeping bags, a camp stove, a few pots and pans. That was it. The cabin echoed with emptiness.

But word got out. Somehow, people in Estes Park heard that a single mom and her kids had moved into town with nothing—and they started showing up.

The first items to arrive were bunk beds and mattresses for the boys. Then came dressers, dishes, pots, and pans.

I stocked the kitchen with other essentials from the thrift store.

But me? I had a mattress—if you could call it that.

The special dumpster treasure we'd hauled in the day before sat in my empty bedroom, old and lumpy, definitely questionable.

But after weeks of sleeping in the truck and months before that on a shelter cot, I didn't care. That first night, when I finally lay down on it, it felt like the Ritz-Carlton.

One person's trash really was another person's treasure.

For a few weeks, which became my nightly routine: coming home exhausted from Safeway shifts and collapsing onto my salvaged mattress, grateful for anything softer than the truck bed or a hardwood floor.

Then a woman I'd met through work made me an offer I couldn't refuse—her brand-new mattress and box spring.

She'd purchased it but wasn't satisfied with the firmness and was willing to sell it to me far below value, along with a dresser.

Best purchase I'd ever made.

With the boys' help again, we loaded my dumpster treasure back onto the truck and returned it to where we'd found it—hoping it might help someone else the way it had helped me.

Full circle. From trash to treasure and back to trash again.

Slowly, our empty cabin became a home.

A table appeared. Chairs followed. A couch someone no longer needed.

Each piece was a gift, a reminder that even when you have nothing, kindness still exists.

Then, in late September, something unexpected happened: a lump-sum back payment arrived from child support.

I'd been receiving sporadic payments from Ron over the years, sometimes a little, sometimes nothing at all. California had garnished his wages when they could, but it was inconsistent at best.

When we moved to Colorado, the case transferred to a new system, and somehow, in the bureaucratic shuffle, they discovered he owed thousands in back payments.

The check that arrived wasn't huge, but to me, it felt like winning the lottery.

For the first time since we arrived, I could replace the things we'd lost to theft back in California. I picked up a basic television so my children could enjoy watching movies on our VCR.

A microwave, so we didn't have to heat everything on the stove. A toaster. Small appliances that made daily life a little bit easier.

I stood in our little cabin, surrounded by the furniture that had been given to us, the thrift-store finds, and now these few new things—and I felt something shift inside me.

We'd done it.

Against all odds, we'd built a life.

One night, as I lay in bed in our little cabin—a real bed, in a real house, with my kids safe in the next room—I thought about everything we'd been through: the welfare lines, the broken system, the shelter's rigid rules, the camping trailer with no bathroom, the nine weeks of moving from campground to campground, the hardwood floor that bruised my hips, the dumpster mattress that felt like luxury.

And I realized—we hadn't just survived.

We'd built something.

Not because everything was perfect. Not because we had everything we needed.

But because we refused to give up.

We kept moving forward, one exhausting day at a time, trusting that God would provide—and He had.

From welfare to wilderness.

From surviving to thriving.

We were home.

And I thought that meant things would finally calm down.

Bless my optimistic little heart.

This is where life politely taps me on the shoulder and says,

"Sit down, sweetheart. I'm not done with you yet."

Chapter 14
Finding My Place (Again)

One night, as I lay in bed in our little home, I prayed and felt something I hadn't experienced in a while a deep sense of contentment, peace that settled over me like a warm blanket.

No more counting days until we had to pack up and move. No more wondering where we'd sleep next week. No more lying awake calculating how to stretch five dollars into three meals.

Just stillness. Just peace.

I immersed myself in hiking and camping, savoring the beauty of our surroundings. Meanwhile, my kids found part-time jobs around town, which became full-time during the summer months. These experiences helped them gain independence and learn to manage their own needs.

I only worked at Safeway for a couple of weeks. It wasn't a bad job, but it wasn't where I was supposed to be. I could feel it. So I started applying to other places—shops down in the valley, offices, anywhere that was hiring. But one place kept calling me back.

The YMCA.

At first, I hesitated. Mom worked there, and despite our improving relationship, I still craved independence.

I didn't want to be seen as the woman who got a job because her mother worked there. I wanted to prove I could make it on my own.

But the YMCA kept calling. And the more I thought about it, the more it made sense. Mom was happy there. The benefits were good. The kids had already spent their days there. And honestly, we were getting along well. Maybe it was time to let go of my need to keep distance between us.

I applied.

The interview went well, and I was hired as a seasonal housekeeper. It felt like a small victory—not a glamorous job, but it was mine. And then, almost immediately, they promoted me to full-time housekeeping supervisor.

I was stunned.

Me? A supervisor? I'd spent years being told I wasn't capable enough, good enough. And now I was being trusted to lead a team?

It felt surreal.

And here's the thing that made it even better: Mom worked in the kitchen. I worked in housekeeping. Completely different departments. We barely saw each other during the workday. I had my independence after all.

My first day as a supervisor, I was terrified.

There were five supervisors in total, managing over 100 employees. Most of them were college students—young, energetic, and full of life. And me? I was a shy, divorced single mom who'd crawled out of homelessness a few months earlier.

Each supervisor was responsible for about 20 employees, and each crew rotated daily.

My team changed constantly, which meant meeting new people, learning new personalities, and trying to figure out how to lead without feeling like an imposter.

But something unexpected happened: those college kids broke through my shyness.

They were outgoing, adventurous, and eager to be in the mountains. They wanted to be there just as much as I did.

And the work—while hard, with long hours and grueling tasks—became something we did together, laughing our way through it.

I quickly learned that the best way to survive those long days was to have fun.

I started bringing an ice chest filled with sodas and snacks. We'd take breaks, sit in the sun, and joke about the absurdity of scrubbing toilets in paradise. The work was exhausting, but we spent more time laughing than complaining. And somehow, that made all the difference.

What made it even more special was the diversity of the staff. The YMCA attracted international students from all over the world—Hungary, Ukraine, Germany, Russia, Mexico, and beyond. These young people had traveled thousands of miles to work in the Rocky Mountains, and their stories were incredible.

One evening, I invited eight of them over to my little cabin for pizza.

We crammed around my small table—a man from Hungary, one from Ukraine, a woman from Germany, someone from Russia, another from Mexico—and we talked for hours. They shared stories about their countries, their families, their dreams.

I listened, fascinated, realizing how small my world had been and how much bigger it was becoming.

After work, we'd all go skating at the indoor rink or find a place to hang out together. For the first time in years, I had friends. Real friends. People who saw me not as a struggling single mom or a welfare case, but as someone worth knowing, worth spending time with. And the YMCA provided free meals for employees, which was a lifesaver.

Between the steady income and not having to worry about feeding myself during the day, I finally felt like I could breathe.

At home, things were… mostly good.

Jason and Heidi were adjusting to school well. They'd made friends, joined activities, and seemed genuinely happy. But Jacob? Jacob was a different story.

He hated Estes Park. He hated the move. And he hated me for bringing him here.

Every day, the kids got home a few minutes before I did. And every day, as soon as I pulled into the driveway, I'd see Jacob sprint to his bedroom and climb into bed, pretending to be asleep.

He ignored me completely.

At night, I'd go to bed, and he'd get up—deliberately avoiding me, making sure we never had to be in the same room. This went on for days. Weeks, even.

On weekends, he'd disappear—off riding his bike, off exploring, off anywhere that wasn't home. I knew he was angry. I knew he blamed me for taking him away from his life in California, from his friends, from everything familiar.

And I didn't know how to fix it.

At night, I lay awake, wondering if I'd made a terrible mistake. Wondering if I'd ruined his life by dragging him to Colorado. Wondering if he'd ever forgive me.

So I gave him space. I showed up, stayed present, and hoped that eventually, time would do what my words couldn't.

But I also knew this: staying in California would have broken all of us. And as much as it hurt to watch Jacob struggle, I had to believe that eventually, he'd see what I saw—that this place, this life, was worth the pain of starting over.

I also learned about a local organization that aided families. Expecting only a small bag of food, like I had received in California, I was shocked at the generosity of this town. They provided vouchers for all four of us to buy hiking boots at a sporting goods store, which later came in handy during the snow. They also gave me gas vouchers for the truck and weekly invitations to eat at a local restaurant for free—even letting my mom join us. On top of that, they provided weekly baskets of food.

As Christmas approached, the blessings continued. Employees at work began giving wrapped Christmas presents to my children, and before I knew it, gifts were left in the front of my truck after my shifts. I'd come home to find presents stacked on our doorstep. The front room quickly filled with so many gifts that my kids had more than they'd ever had in their lives. I even wondered where I would store them all.

One day, I returned home from work to find a Christmas tree on our porch—another gift, this time from the manager at Safeway.

I also received a voucher for a cord of firewood to keep warm during the winter months.

Work was especially busy during the holiday season. The school district only allowed one week off for Christmas but gave the kids two weeks off for Easter vacation.

Since we had arrived in Estes Park with the camper on our truck and a small trailer holding our belongings, I needed to return to California to retrieve the rest of our items from storage. I worked overtime to cover the cost of renting a truck for the trip. A very kind gentleman I worked for even offered me his credit card to pay for gas for the round trip.

I was in awe of how God had truly moved in our lives through the kindness of this town. During all the years I had been on welfare in California, I longed to get off it, to have the opportunity to work and support my family. But being stuck in that system never allowed for it. Once we moved here, I became self-sufficient and no longer needed welfare. God was blessing me in many ways—through my work, through the kindness of others, and through the sheer beauty of our new home.

This was all I had ever wanted back in California: a little boost and a job to support my family.

On Christmas morning, I watched Jason, Heidi, and even Jacob—who'd been so angry, so distant—tear into those gifts with wide eyes and genuine smiles. And I cried. Not because we'd been given charity, but because we'd been given community—because people had seen us, really seen us, and decided we were worth caring about.

That first winter in Estes Park was magical.

The snow fell thick and heavy, transforming the town into a winter wonderland. It was a different kind of snow than I'd grown up with in the Southern California mountains—lighter, fluffier, deeper. And it made everything feel like an adventure.

Someone from the community donated a cord of wood for our fireplace, and we'd sit around it in the evenings, the warmth wrapping around us like a blanket. I'd put chains on the truck and drive to work through snow-packed roads, feeling like I was living in a postcard.

But what made that winter truly special wasn't the snow. It was the people.

Word had spread around town that a single mom and her kids had moved to Estes Park with almost nothing. And just like when we first arrived, people showed up.

There was a program in town for families who needed help, and we qualified. Through that program, we received not only food, but vouchers for boots, gas, and other essentials. Once a week, we received complimentary meals at nearby restaurants, which seemed almost unreal after relying on food stamps for years.

That winter, for the first time in my life, I understood what it meant to truly belong somewhere.

As the snow melted and spring began to creep into the mountains, I realized something profound: I wasn't just surviving anymore.

I had a job I loved, surrounded by people who made me laugh. I had a home—small, but ours. I had a community that had wrapped its arms around us and refused to let go.

And my kids? Jason was flourishing. Heidi was happy. Even Jacob—though still angry—was slowly, so slowly, beginning to soften.

We had made it through the hardest part. The camping. The moving. The uncertainty. The fear that we'd fail, that I'd made a terrible mistake, that we'd end up right back where we started.

But we hadn't failed. We'd built something. Piece by piece, day by day, laugh by laugh.

I'd spent years being told I wasn't enough. Not educated enough for college. Not capable enough for the Navy. Not worthy enough for help when I needed it most.

In this mountain town, among caring strangers, I proved them all wrong. I was enough. I'd always been enough.

And for the first time in my life, I believed it.

Within a year, we moved out of the small two-bedroom cabin and into a larger three-bedroom home on the lake.

Everything was finally falling into place—our home, my job, the kids… even Jacob was slowly unfurling from his teenage scowl. But peace never stays too long in my story.

So grab a snack and turn the page, because that's where things start getting interesting.

Chapter 15
Roots

Jacob softened.

It didn't happen overnight. There was no dramatic moment, no movie scene where he suddenly forgave me and hugged me and everything was magically fixed. But slowly, over that first year, I started to see glimpses of the kid he used to be—the one who laughed easily, talked nonstop, and wasn't angry at the world.

The turning point came when he met a friend at school who loved music as much as he did.

Jacob had drumsticks but no drum. His friend had a drum but no drumsticks. It was fate. They bonded instantly, and suddenly Jacob had someone who understood him, someone who didn't think music was noise but life. From there, other friendships followed.

And just like that, he became popular. Really popular.

The angry kid who'd spent months avoiding me was now joining activities, making friends, and finding his place. He still wasn't quick to forgive me for uprooting his life, but he no longer sprinted to his room when I walked through the door.

It was progress. And I'd take it.

I was thriving too.

At the YMCA, I found more than a job—I found a community. Three women became my closest friends: Viki, Linda, and JoAnn.

All of us were single, navigating life on our own terms, and we decided that if we were going to do this, we might as well do it together.

Once a month, we'd plan an outing.

We took turns organizing something—dinner at a nice restaurant, a trip to a dinner theater, or a Valentine's Day celebration where we toasted to ourselves instead of waiting for someone else to make us feel special.

Those outings were a lifeline.

They reminded me that I wasn't just a mom or an employee or someone trying to hold everything together. I was still a person—with friends, interests, and a life beyond survival.

The YMCA also gave employees complimentary cabin stays each year, and I took full advantage.

Whenever friends or family visited, I'd rent the biggest cabin I could get. We hiked, explored, and sat around the fire at night like we were finally living the life we used to only dream about.

Those cabins were proof of how far we'd come—
from camping in a tent with no bathroom
to hosting guests in a mountain lodge.

After a year in the tiny two-bedroom cabin, I moved us into a bigger three-bedroom place right across from the lake.

It was bright and spacious, and for the first time, Heidi had her own room. No more cramming into tiny spaces. We had room to breathe—room to live.

We had finally arrived.

The kids were finding their own rhythms in Estes Park.

Heidi, always independent, went to summer camp her first year. I thought she'd love it—outdoors, friends, freedom. She hated it. I mean, she absolutely hated it. She came home early and announced she was getting a job instead.

She was twelve.

She got hired at a downtown deli, earning her own money and riding to work on an old bicycle I'd fixed up.

I didn't have the right paint, so I used whatever I had. It wasn't pretty, but it worked.

One day, she visited me at work and parked it outside the break room.

When my crew walked by, someone asked, laughing, "Oh my God, whose ugly bike is that?"

I kept walking like I'd never seen that bike in my life.

Heidi shot me a look, and we smiled and kept moving.

Eventually, I bought her a new bike—a nice one.

But part of her was proud of the ugly one. It was hers. She earned it.

Jason was quieter.

He didn't chase friends or crowds. But he loved to fish. On his days off, he'd head to the lakes and streams and spend hours casting lines. And he was good at it. He'd come home with strings of trout, beaming. Those dinners ranked among our most memorable—not because of the sophistication of the meal, but because he had personally caught it.

The boys got jobs at a local amusement park with go-karts and mini golf.

The best part? After hours, the owners let us run the go-karts ourselves. Just us. We'd race around the track, hollering like kids, the wind slapping our faces. Pure joy.

Each of my kids was carving their own life.

Jacob with his music.

Heidi with her fierce independence.

Jason with his quiet love of the outdoors.

And me? I was grateful just to watch them grow.

Even though we'd once lived in campgrounds, we never stopped loving the outdoors.

Camping became fun again—a choice, not survival.

One weekend, Jason pitched his tent alone while Heidi and I shared one.

Bears had been spotted in the area recently, and all night I worried one would wander into camp. I put a portable radio between our tents, turned it on, and hoped the noise would scare anything away.

It worked. No bears.

But none of us slept a wink with that radio blaring.

We were safe, tired, and laughing by morning.

Later, we took a trail that looked easy on the map.

We hiked up, ate lunch on the rocks, and felt the mountain magic. Then we realized we were miles from the truck. The boys raced ahead to get it while Heidi, her friend Kara, and I limped along the highway. At one point, Heidi's feet hurt so badly she took off her shoes and hid them in a bush, planning to grab them later.

We never found those shoes again.

Somewhere in Colorado, a hiker probably still tells the story of "the mystery shoes in the bushes."

When I wasn't hiking with the kids, I hiked alone.

Once, exhausted after a long climb, I fell asleep on a warm rock by a lake. I woke to something nudging my feet.

My heart stopped.

Bear.

This is it. This is the end.

I opened my eyes—and found ducks.

Just a bunch of ducks poking at my shoes.

Note to self: pick nap spots more wisely.

My sister Louanne visited often.

We hiked, told stories around the fire, and soaked in how far we'd come. She'd seen me at my lowest back in California. Now she could see what I'd built.

But the person who became most important to me was Megan, the YMCA office manager.

We hiked for miles, talking about life. She was a teacher—kind, patient—and she became my English mentor. I had struggled with grammar and vocabulary for years, always convinced I wasn't smart enough. Megan never made me feel that way. She corrected me gently, assigned me homework, and encouraged me endlessly.

She taught me how I could learn.

I could grow.

And slowly, I did.

As the kids grew older, our schedules drifted apart.

They worked. I worked. We were like ships passing in the night—under the same roof but rarely together.

I missed us.

But I didn't know how to fix it.

Then one day, Jacob walked in with football tickets.

Bronco's tickets. Good ones. And he wanted all of us to go—together.

I wasn't a football fan. Still isn't.

But Jacob wanted us there, so we went. For the first time in months, we were together—laughing, cheering (or pretending to), just being a family.

Jacob smiled that day.

A real smile. And when he looked at me during one of the touchdowns—or whatever happened, I saw something I hadn't seen in a long time.

Contentment.

We had made it.

Not perfectly. Not without scars. But we made it.

Later, watching the boys fight over the TV remote, trading "shut ups" until a Broncos game came on—when suddenly they were allies—I realized something:

We weren't just living in Estes Park.

We belonged here.

I worked at the YMCA for five years—five years of supervising crews, making friends, learning English, hiking mountains, and watching my children become themselves.

Those years weren't perfect.

There were setbacks, doubts, and moments I felt like I didn't measure up. But now I see it clearly:

Those years were the foundation.

The stability.

The proof that we could build something real.

I had always believed I would never amount to anything.

But I was wrong.

We weren't just surviving anymore.

We were thriving.

We were rooted.

And my kids and I were just getting started.

We had built a home, a life, and a future.

But even the strongest roots get tested. And mine were about to face something I never saw coming.

Chapter 16
When Doors Close

When Jason's twentieth birthday came around, Heidi and I decorated the house and had presents waiting for him. But he spent the whole day out with his new girlfriend.

I wanted him home—selfishly, if I'm honest. When he finally walked through the door late that evening, the words slipped out before I could stop them.

"You spent your whole birthday out. I decorated. I bought presents. I guess we don't matter anymore."

The look on his face—hurt mixed with frustration—told me instantly I'd crossed a line. I was guilt-tripping him, tugging on a rope that should've been let go a long time ago.

The next morning, his room was empty.

The TV from the front room was gone. His clothes were gone.

Jason had moved out.

My heart sank—not just because he was gone, but because I knew exactly why. I'd tried to keep him tethered to childhood when he was already stepping into adulthood. My fear of losing him had pushed him out the door faster than anything else ever could.

He soon married his girlfriend.

Over the next few years, Jacob and Heidi graduated high school, met their soulmates, and stepped into their own lives.

Before I knew it, the house that once buzzed with noise and chaos became still, and I felt the sting of empty-nest syndrome settle in.

As parents, especially single parents, so much of our identity is wrapped around our kids. We pour ourselves out day after day, wondering if we're doing enough, wondering how we'll make it another week. And then suddenly, the house is quiet, their rooms are empty, and you're left blinking in the stillness, realizing your story hasn't ended—it's shifting.

I remember coming home from work one night, and the silence hit me like a wave. No backpacks dropped by the door. No laughter. No shoes kicked off in the corner. Not even a stray soda can on the table.

Nothing in the house moved.

I confided in a close friend about how lost I felt. She looked at me and said,

"Laurie, your story isn't over. You raised your kids. Now it's time to discover what God has next. You're more than a mom. You're His child—and He's not finished writing your story."

Those words changed everything. This wasn't an ending. It was the beginning of a new season.

If you're reading this from your own empty nest—feeling the ache, the silence, the uncertainty—hear this: God is with you in every season (Ecclesiastes 3:1).

This season, too, carries purpose. Whether it leads to new callings, new relationships, new adventures, or the courage to finish the book inside you (like I eventually did), your life is still full of possibility.

Still, faith doesn't always erase feelings. My closest friend moved away. Most of the people I had built connections within Estes Park had left as well. It was always a transient town—beautiful, but temporary for most. As people moved on, one by one, I looked around and realized I was the only one left.

The house wasn't empty because the kids were gone; it was empty because nothing remained of them. Just me and quiet.

At first, I tried to outrun the loneliness with busyness—cleaning, organizing, working extra hours. But the silence followed.

So, I started walking.

Every evening after work, I laced up my shoes and headed into the woods, down the same trails where my kids once ran ahead of me, laughing and carefree. Now those trails held only my footsteps and my prayers.

I talked out loud to God—because, honestly, who else was there to listen?

Why did this season feel so heavy?

What am I supposed to do now?

Where did I fit?

The answers didn't come quickly, but they came slowly, quietly, like the rustling of leaves. Somewhere along those winding paths, I realized I wasn't walking alone. God had been with me through every storm, every survival, every joy—and He was still with me now.

One evening, with the sun setting behind the peaks, I stopped mid-trail.

For the first time, the quiet didn't feel like punishment.

It felt like invitation.

An invitation to rediscover who I was.

To dream again.

To believe God wasn't finished with me—not by a long shot.

My walks became less about escaping loneliness and more about meeting God in it.

With each step, I found strength.

With each breath, I found hope.

With each prayer, I felt a new chapter forming in the distance.

But believing that the best was ahead and being able to live it—those were two different things.

The three-bedroom house I once filled with love and chaos had become a financial burden I couldn't carry alone. Rent, which once seemed manageable, now felt impossible. I'd sit at the kitchen table with bills spread out in front of me, doing the math repeatedly, praying the numbers would magically change.

They never did.

Reality was closing in.

Something had to give.

When everything felt like it was falling apart, God was quietly setting the stage for what came next.

A new chapter.

A new purpose.

A new beginning I never could've predicted

Chapter 17
From Struggle to Strength

The house by the lake in Estes Park was perfect when we first moved in. Three bedrooms, enough space for all of us, windows that looked out on the water. For a while, it felt like we'd finally made it—a real home, stable job, the kids thriving. But houses have a way of changing size depending on who's in them.

Jason was the first to leave, and he did it without warning. He'd been spending more time on the computer, chatting with someone he'd met online. A girl in Denver. I'd ask him about her, and he'd grin that mischievous grin of his and change the subject. Jason had always been funny—quick with a joke, able to make me laugh even on the hardest days.

But I noticed he wasn't coming home as much. He'd stay out late, sleep somewhere else, show up for dinner, and then disappear again. Then one day, I came home from work and walked into the living room. Something didn't feel right.

The TV was gone.

We'd all been sharing that one piece of entertainment in the whole house. And now there was an empty spot on the stand, a dust outline where it used to be. That's when I realized: Jason hadn't just gone out. He'd moved out.

I went to his room. Empty. Closet cleaned out. Fishing gear gone. Boots were gone. Every trace of him packed up and taken to Denver while I was at work. No conversation. No "Mom, I think I'm ready to move out." No chance to say goodbye properly.

Just gone.

I stood in his empty room and tried not to cry. He was nineteen—old enough to make his own choices. And he was in love, head over heels, ready to start his own life. I couldn't blame him for that. But it still hurt.

When he finally called a few days later, I tried to keep my voice steady.

"I'm in Denver, Mom," he said, and I could hear the excitement in his voice. "I'll visit."

"Okay," I said. "I'm happy for you."

And I was. But I was also heartbroken.

Jacob graduated high school in 1999. By then, he'd completely forgiven me for dragging him to Colorado. He'd found his music, his friends, his place. He got his own apartment in town and threw himself into work and life.

"You did good, Mom," he told me the day he moved out. "I'm glad we came here."

I held onto those words like a lifeline.

Heidi left in 2000. She'd always been my independent one, my fighter. She found work and her own place, and just like that, she was gone too.

The three-bedroom house suddenly felt enormous.

And expensive.

I did the math repeatedly, hoping the numbers would somehow change. They never did. The rent that had felt manageable when the kids were home and I was working overtime now loomed over me like a weight I couldn't carry. Between rent, utilities, and gas to get to work, I would barely break even each month.

I tried to convince myself I'd be fine. I still worked at the YMCA. I still hiked the trails. I still had my routine.

But the house echoed. Every footstep sounded too loud. Every night, I'd come home to silence—no music playing, no arguing over the TV remote, no laughter. Just me and the empty rooms.

This is too much space, I thought. I need to downsize.

So I did. I moved into a small one-bedroom apartment, thinking that less space would mean less loneliness and lower rent would mean breathing room in my budget.

I was wrong on both counts.

The apartment wasn't cozy; it was stifling. Instead of feeling manageable, it amplified the loneliness I was already grappling with. Without the familiar comfort of my old home, I felt unmoored, as if I had lost not just a house but a piece of my identity.

At least in the house, I could tell myself the kids were just in their rooms, just out with friends, just temporarily gone. But in that tiny apartment, there was nowhere to hide from the truth:

I was alone.

I'd come home from work and stand in the doorway, staring at the four walls that felt more like a cell than a home. The silence pressed in on me from all sides.

God, the silence was deafening.

The "could haves" and "should haves" played endlessly in my mind. Maybe I could have found another way to keep the house. Maybe I should have tried harder. Maybe I'd given up the last piece of stability I had.

Living in that small apartment only deepened my sense of isolation. The walls that had once symbolized a fresh start now felt suffocating, closing in no matter how hard I tried to fill the silence.

Working at the YMCA wasn't much better. Business was slowing down, and the workplace dynamic had changed. The new hires were younger, fresh out of school, and while they were friendly enough, I struggled to connect with them.

Our life experiences were worlds apart, making conversations feel superficial. The camaraderie I once shared with my older coworkers was gone, and with it, the sense of belonging I had relied on.

One by one, my friends had moved on—Megan, my hiking partner and English tutor; Viki; Linda; and JoAnn, my partners in crime. They'd all left for new jobs, new cities, new chapters of their lives.

And I was still here.

Stuck.

Alone.

Even Mom had relocated to the area and was staying at Deanna's house on her days off while she worked as a seasonal employee at the Grand Canyon.

By early 2002, I'd wake up in the mornings and realize something terrifying: I know no one in this town anymore. Not a single person. Everyone I'd built relationships with for over six years had left. The town was full of people, but I was invisible. I'd go to the grocery store, the post office, the library—and never see a familiar face.

It was like living in a ghost town where I was the only ghost.

I wasn't just sad, I was sinking.

The depression crept in slowly at first, then swallowed me whole. Some mornings, I could barely get out of bed. Work became mechanical—go through the motions, smile when you're supposed to, go home. Hiking, which had always been my therapy, felt hollow. Even prayer felt like shouting into a void.

Desperate for relief, I reached out for help. The mental health department prescribed a strong antidepressant, assuring me it would lift the fog I was drowning in. But instead of easing the pain, it dulled everything. I felt disconnected, even from the small moments of peace I had once cherished. I didn't feel like myself anymore.

So I made the decision to stop taking the medication. I believed I was doing the right thing—taking control of my healing. To explain my decision, I wrote a letter to my doctor, carefully outlining my reasons. I wasn't trying to avoid the pain; I wanted to face it in a way that felt real.

But I didn't expect the response that followed.

The doctor's office placed me on suicide watch. I understood why they did it, but it felt like an overreaction. The truth was, I wasn't suicidal. I wasn't thinking about ending my life. I was overwhelmed, struggling to find a way out of the deep well of sadness I was in. I wasn't asking for a way out of life; I was searching for a way back to myself—to breathe again, to feel like I had a purpose beyond the walls of that apartment.

The watch period passed. The fog didn't lift overnight, but slowly—so slowly I barely noticed—I started looking for small ways forward.

Hiking became my therapy again. At first, it was about putting one foot in front of the other, letting the rhythm of my steps drown out the noise in my mind.

One day, while on a solo hike, I realized I had accidentally taken a "shortcut"—the kind where you end up further from your car than when you started. As I stood there with my map upside down, debating whether to laugh or cry, I decided to laugh. That moment was the beginning of my rediscovery of humor and lightness.

I joined a senior hiking group, even though I was only in my 40s. The silver-haired adults could outwalk me without breaking a sweat while I huffed and puffed, trying to keep up. It became a running joke in the group that I was their "junior member in training." These moments of shared laughter and camaraderie reminded me that life is messy, unpredictable, and sometimes hilariously imperfect, but it's still worth every step on the trail.

Slowly, through these small but meaningful adventures, I found my way back to hope.

But even then, I still couldn't manage living on my own. My kids were busy with their lives, and I didn't seem to fit into their schedules. The apartment that was supposed to save me money felt like it was costing me my sanity.

Then one evening, the phone rang.

"Hey," Deanna's voice came through, bright and warm. "How are you?"

"I'm fine," I lied automatically.

There was a pause. "You don't sound fine."

I broke. Standing in my too-small apartment, phone pressed to my ear, I told her everything—the loneliness, the depression, the sense that I'd completely lost myself. The fact that I didn't know a single person in town anymore.

"Come stay with me," she said without hesitation. "Mom is here too. I've got a house on a 400-acre ranch. It's quiet and peaceful. I've got horses, goats, all sorts of animals. You can help me with the farm, clear your head. Come for a few weeks. See how you feel."

I looked around my tiny apartment. At the walls that felt like they were closing in. At the silence that had become unbearable.

"Are there spiders?" I asked.

Deanna laughed. "Not the big California kind."

"Okay," I heard myself say. "I'll come."

Two weeks later, I loaded up my truck with everything I thought I'd need for what I told myself would be a month-long visit—

clothes, camping gear, and a few books I'd probably be too tired to read anyway. I'd already turned in my notice at work and stuffed the rest of my belongings into storage.

As I pulled away from Estes Park, I checked the rearview mirror one last time. This town had seen me raise three kids on my own, build a life from scratch, and somehow keep going when everything told me to quit. But that chapter was over.

The drive to Utah felt endless. Each mile stretched longer than the last, my body aching in the seat, my mind wrestling with doubt. Am I running away again? Will I ever stop running?

But as the landscape shifted from Colorado mountains to Utah desert, something unexpected happened. The openness of the land, the vast sky, the sense of space, it didn't feel like running. It felt like breathing.

By the time I crossed into Utah, the sun was setting, painting the desert in shades of orange and gold. I rolled down my window and let the warm air rush in.

Maybe this wasn't running. Maybe this was moving forward.

And maybe—just maybe—somewhere on that farm with Deanna, I'd learn how to do more than survive.

I didn't know what waited for me in the next chapter—only that life was about to throw me another curveball. And knowing my track record, I'd probably try to catch it with my face.

But hey… that's where the good stories usually begin.

Chapter 18
Embracing New Horizons

The drive from Estes Park to southern Utah took eleven hours. By the time I finally pulled onto Deanna's property, the sun had long since slipped below the horizon. It was well past bedtime, and exhaustion pressed down on me—physical fatigue from the drive, emotional exhaustion from everything I'd just left behind.

I barely managed to grab some clothes from the truck before stumbling inside and collapsing into bed.

As soon as morning comes, I'm leaving, I thought as my head hit the pillow. This was a mistake. I'll go back to Colorado and figure something else out.

The plan was clear: at the first hint of dawn, turn the truck around and head back to... what? An empty apartment where I knew no one?

I fell asleep before I could finish the thought.

The First Morning

The first morning on the farm was an assault on my senses.

Gone were the crisp alpine air and towering pines of Colorado. Instead, I woke to the scent of hay, the distant moos of cows, a handful of unfamiliar farm smells—and a rooster who seemed determined to make sure no one on earth ever slept past dawn again.

I pulled a pillow over my head. Nope. I'm leaving.

But then Deanna's voice called from the kitchen.

"Coffee's ready!"

Dragging myself from bed, I found her already dressed and cheerful—as if being woken up by a rooster with anger issues was perfectly normal.

"I think I might head back today—" I began.

"Just stay a little longer," she said gently. "I promise you won't regret it."

Those words hung in the air.

I looked out the window at sagebrush stretching endlessly toward distant mountains. Colorado was familiar. This place was… different.

But something in me hesitated.

"Just a few more days," Deanna said. "Help me with the horses. Get your bearings."

And before I could stop myself, I said, "Okay. A few more days."

Those few days turned into weeks, and weeks into months. What followed was a season of unexpected transformation—one that revealed layers of resilience and strength I'd forgotten I had.

Learning the Farm

I started by following Deanna around, learning the routines. She rode a spirited, unpredictable horse; I got Ivan—a steady, twenty-five-year-old gentleman who moved at a beginner-safe crawl.

"Ivan's a gentleman," Deanna said, patting his neck. "He'll take care of you."

And he did. Ivan became my therapy, my companion, my reminder that steadiness still existed.

But farm life wasn't all peaceful trail rides.

It was wild, messy, and unpredictable. Stubborn goats. Ill-tempered pigs. Horses who behaved perfectly until they didn't. And that rooster—always that rooster—who seemed to take personal offense at the idea of me sleeping in

There were lambs, cows, and enough daily chaos to make me regularly question my life choices.

But nothing tested my patience like the pigs.

One afternoon, I was strolling around the yard on the cordless phone with my friend Megan when I saw a pig outside its pen. No big deal, I thought.

Until he started charging straight at me.

Panicking, I sprinted to the truck and scrambled into the back just in time. Still holding the phone, I watched as the pig circled the truck like a pink, snorting shark.

"What is wrong with you? Shoo! Go away!" I yelled.

"Laurie… are you okay?" Megan asked, trying not to laugh.

"I'm being held hostage by a pig," I said flatly.

After several minutes of circling, the pig seemed to lose interest. Cautiously, I jumped down.

Big mistake.

He spun around and charged again. I barely made it onto the porch, slamming the screen door behind me.

He stood there, snorting at me through the screen like a farmyard bouncer.

That was the day I lost all respect for pigs.

And then there were the days of feeding the horses twice a day. It became my first real responsibility. In exchange for helping care for the animals, Deanna and I received meat from the owners—a simple barter system that worked beautifully.

With Deanna working in town most days, I was often alone on the farm. But unlike in Colorado, the solitude didn't feel suffocating. Out here, alone, I didn't feel lonely; it felt peaceful.

Through an ad in the local newspaper, I landed work with a company installing streetlights. The pay was double what I'd earned in Colorado, and with almost no expenses, I finally began saving money.

Then Old Ivan died.

I found out one morning. He'd passed quietly in the pasture overnight. Standing over the place where he'd been found, I felt a quiet grief—not the sobbing kind, but the kind that sits in your chest for a long time.

Ivan had given me exactly what I needed when I needed it. And now he was gone.

I never rode again.

Watching Deanna get thrown from her feisty mare only confirmed my fears. No horse would ever replace Ivan.

Farm life continued, though something had shifted. The animals remained, the routines stayed the same, but Ivan's absence left a space nothing else quite filled. Still, there was work to be done. Weekdays were for work, weekends for exploring. Cedar Breaks was fifteen miles away; Bryce Canyon was only thirteen. The Colorado beauty I'd left behind was slowly being replaced by a different kind of majesty.

As winter approached, I helped Deanna and one of her friend's cut firewood in the hills. The area was nicknamed "Little Alaska" for a reason—winters were long, brutal, and cold.

The house was a small two-bedroom. I shared a room with Deanna at first, but within a few weeks, we cleared the basement and turned it into my room, my quiet sanctuary. The nearest city with Walmart and Home Depot was eighty-nine miles away. Deanna made the weekly trip; I stayed home to tend the animals. She loved thrift shopping, and I'd wake up to find little treasures—Levi's jeans or shirts—neatly placed on the stairs.

Life developed a rhythm. Work. Weekends. Evenings spent reading or walking the property. It wasn't exciting, but it was steady.

And steady was exactly what I needed.

One night, completely alone on the farm, the silence was absolute—except for one lonely lamb bleating into the darkness. There was no moon, and the night was so black I couldn't see my own hand.

I opened the door but could see nothing.

"You're okay, little guy," I whispered into the dark. "Go to sleep. You'll find your mama in the morning."

The bleating stopped instantly.

The night fell silent, as if he'd taken comfort in my words.

Healing in Small, Unexpected Ways

Adjusting wasn't easy. I'd resisted the mornings, the animals, the chaos. But slowly, the resistance chipped away.

The farm wasn't keeping me busy.

It was healing me.

Morning walks became my prayer time. At first, it was just me and the cat, who followed faithfully. Then one morning, I felt watched. My heart pounded—until I turned and found a llama staring at me.

Eventually, I led a small parade of animals on my daily walks.

Then came the mud incident. I wandered too close to a pond, stepped onto what I thought was solid ground, and instantly sank into thick mud—face first.

For a moment, I was convinced I was being swallowed by quicksand.

I clawed my way out, covered head to toe in mud, and as I stumbled back toward the house, the cows took one look at me and bolted like they'd seen a ghost.

Even I had to laugh.

Some nights, when sleep wouldn't come, I walked into the pasture and prayed beneath the stars. I always returned feeling lighter, as if God met me right there in the field.

One late fall afternoon, I stopped by the post office and noticed a flyer:

NATIONAL PARK SERVICE — SEASONAL POSITIONS AVAILABLE

Something stirred inside me.

Memories of childhood summers. Yosemite. Yellowstone. The Grand Canyon. The freedom of wild places.

I could do that, I thought. I could work in a national park.

The farm had steadied me. It healed me. But standing there in that tiny post office, I felt the pull toward something more.

That evening, I showed the flyer to Deanna.

"Are you going to apply?" she asked. "This is right up your alley."

"Why not?" I said. "Let's see how to do it."

We looked it up, and one morning, I sat at her kitchen table with coffee and a stack of applications printed from the library. I filled out everyone—Yellowstone, Yosemite, Grand Canyon, Zion, Bryce Canyon. Parks west of the Mississippi and a few back east, too.

I stuffed them into bright yellow envelopes and drove to the post office.

"Big plans?" the clerk asked with a smile.

"Maybe," I said. "We'll see."

Driving back to the farm, I felt something rise in me.

Hope.

Not desperate hope. Not fragile hope. But the kind of hope that comes after healing.

The kind that whispers: "You're ready!"

The farm had given me that.

The farm had steadied me, but my story wasn't meant to end there. Something new was waiting—and I could finally feel myself walking toward it.

Chapter 19
Yellowstone Bound-Spring 2004

The envelope sat on Deanna's kitchen table, stamped with the words Yellowstone National Park.

I'd been checking the mail obsessively for weeks, telling myself not to get my hopes up. I'd applied to dozens of parks. Maybe I wouldn't hear back from any of them. Maybe seasonal work in national parks was one of those dreams that looked good on paper but never actually happened.

But there it was.

I pulled out the letter and scanned it quickly, my eyes jumping from line to line.

We are pleased to offer you a position…

Maintenance worker…

Housing provided…

Report date: May 15, 2004…

"I got it," I whispered.

"I got it!" I said louder, laughing, almost giddy with joy, holding the letter like it might disappear if I didn't grip it tightly enough.

Deanna beamed. "I told you! I knew you would!"

I sank into a chair. Yellowstone. I was going to work in Yellowstone National Park.

It wasn't a park I had seen before, but it was one I'd dreamed of visiting as a kid with Mom and my grandmother.

Another place of wild spaces and mountains. A place that had always seemed like a different world, beautiful, untouchable, magical.

And now I was going to live there. Work there. Be part of it.

For a moment, everything went quiet. I sat there holding the letter, realizing this was the start of something new. I didn't know what lay ahead, but I knew I was ready.

The next few weeks were a blur of preparation.

I gave notice at the streetlight company. They were sorry to see me go but understood—you don't turn down a job at Yellowstone.

I packed my truck with camping supplies and as many canned goods as I could fit, unsure what would be available once I got there. Deanna helped me load everything, both of us trying not to acknowledge that I was leaving again.

"You'll come back for the winter, right?" she asked the night before I left.

"Of course," I said. "Where else would I go?"

The farm had become home. Not the way Estes Park had been home, or California before that. This place had held me while I was healing, given me space to figure out who I was without the kids, without the constant scramble to survive.

I'd arrived broken and desperate.

I was leaving whole and hopeful.

In the morning, I left, and Deanna stood in the driveway waving as I pulled away. In the rearview mirror, the farm grew smaller—the barn, the pastures, the mountains beyond. The place that had saved me.

But I wasn't sad.

I was ready.

The drive to Yellowstone was supposed to be straightforward. Idaho. Montana. Wyoming. Follow the map, arrive by evening, get settled.

But somewhere in Idaho, I saw a sign for hot springs.

I'd always loved hot springs, the heat, the minerals, the way they relaxed your whole body. After everything I'd been through, a soak felt earned.

Why not? I thought. A perfect way to end the drive.

I veered off the main route, following signs down increasingly rural roads, already imagining the warm water and relaxation.

Twenty minutes later, I pulled up to the hot springs.

Closed.

A handwritten sign on the gate read: Closed for Maintenance. Reopening June 1.

I sat in the truck, staring at it. "Of course," I muttered. "Why would anything be easy?"

Then I laughed. A year ago, this would've ruined my day. Now? It was just another detour—one I'd chosen.

I turned around and got back on the road, now hours behind schedule.

I decided to take the scenic route through Jackson and the Grand Tetons. Towering peaks. Pristine lakes. Valleys that looked like paintings.

But when I reached Yellowstone's southern entrance, I hit another obstacle.

The gate was closed—still snowed in.

That little surprise added another four to five hours, forcing me to loop all the way around to the north entrance. By the time I finally entered the park, the sun was setting, and I was exhausted.

Still, I noticed the landscape changing.

The mountains rose higher. The trees thickened. Wildlife appeared—elk, bison, a fox darting across the road. The air smelled differently, cleaner, wilder, like the world had taken a deep breath and held it.

Eighteen miles beyond the north entrance, winding through valleys and alongside rivers, I finally reached Tower Junction.

It was more remote than I'd imagined.

My seasonal housing sat in a cluster of buildings: four two-bedroom trailers, three small houses, and a bunkhouse.

Forest surrounded everything, mountains rising on all sides. According to my map, the nearest gas station was eighty miles south near Old Faithful.

This is it, I thought, pulling up to my assigned trailer. *This is where I'll be living.*

I was too tired to feel much of anything. I grabbed my bags, found my trailer, and stumbled inside.

A woman looked up from the small kitchen table. She was in her thirties, dark hair pulled into a ponytail, wearing a fleece jacket with a National Park Service patch.

"You must be Laurie," she said, standing and extending her hand. "I'm JoAnn. I work on the wolf project."

"Nice to meet you," I said, shaking her hand. "Sorry I'm so late. Took the scenic route. The very, very scenic route."

She laughed. "No worries. Your room's on the right. Get settled—we'll talk in the morning."

My room was small but clean, with a full-size bed, a dresser, a window overlooking the forest. After years of rougher living, it felt like luxury.

I collapsed onto the bed without unpacking and fell asleep within minutes.

The next morning, sunlight streamed through the window, accompanied by birdsong I didn't recognize.

For a moment, I forgot where I was.

Then it hit me.

Yellowstone.

I walked to the window.

The view stole my breath—towering pines, a valley stretching endlessly, mountains rising beyond. No houses. No roads. Just wilderness.

JoAnn was already up, making coffee.

"Sleep, okay?" she asked.

"Like the dead," I said. "Where's the nearest… anything?"

She laughed. "That's Tower Junction. We're eighteen miles from the entrance, and the nearest town is sixty miles north. For groceries or gas, it's Mammoth Hot Springs—about twenty miles west—or all the way down to Old Faithful."

"Mammoth Hot Springs has a store?"

"Yep. Gas station, grocery store, post office, coffee shop, bookstore. It's the main hub for employees up here."

Relief washed over me. "Why didn't the packet mention that?"

She shrugged. "They assume you'll figure it out. Welcome to the National Park Service."

After breakfast, JoAnn offered to show me around.

"You'll want the lay of the land before they throw you in," she said.

We drove to Mammoth Hot Springs, and with every mile, my spirits lifted. The small cluster of buildings felt like civilization after Tower Junction's isolation.

The store was stocked. The coffee shop had real espresso. The bookstore was charming.

I could survive here.

"See?" JoAnn said. "Not so bad."

That evening, she invited me for a walk.

"Lost Lake," she said. "You in?"

I agreed, expecting a gentle stroll

It was not gentle.

We climbed a steep mountain trail, JoAnn leading with bear spray—until a noise in the bushes stopped her cold.

She froze. Looked at me.

I took the lead. (Apparently, I'm braver when someone else panics first.)

We reached Lost Lake, breathless but rewarded. The water reflected the mountains perfectly, a mirror image that felt unreal.

"Welcome to Yellowstone," JoAnn said. "This is why we're here."

Standing there, I understood.

Chapter 20
Where I'm Supposed to Be

My first official day of work began at 7 a.m. sharp.

I met my supervisor, Tom—a weathered man who looked like he'd been carved from the same stone as the mountains. He introduced me to the rest of the crew: seven other maintenance workers, most of whom had been coming to Yellowstone for years, even decades.

"All right, Spencer," Tom said, glancing at his clipboard. "Let's see what you're made of. Your first assignment is vault toilets."

My heart sank. Of course.

One of the older workers grinned. "We all started there. Consider it a rite of passage."

I was handed rubber gloves, industrial-strength cleaning supplies, and a breathing mask.

"You'll want that," someone said, nodding at the mask.

They weren't wrong.

Vault toilets—essentially fancy outhouses—are a necessary part of any national park. They need to be cleaned, maintained, and restocked with supplies. And after a long winter, they need serious attention.

I'll admit, I was embarrassed at first. Here I was, in one of the most beautiful places on Earth, scrubbing toilets. But as I worked through that first day—and the next, and the next—I realized something important.

It didn't matter what job I was doing. I was doing it here. In Yellowstone.

Where the air was clean. Where eagles soared overhead. Where I could look up from my work and see mountains in every direction.

I was part of something bigger than myself, helping keep the park accessible and beautiful for the millions of visitors who somehow thought bison were big cows.

Vault toilets were just the beginning.

As the weeks went on, the work diversified. I cleared trails, painted buildings, directed traffic around wandering bison, and learned the difference between a curious bear and a dangerous one. (Hint: if it's walking toward you, it's the second kind.)

Mark, an older maintenance worker who'd been at Yellowstone for over twenty years, took me under his wing.

"You've got good hands," he said, watching me repair a fence. "And you're not afraid of hard work. That matters more than experience."

Mark taught me carpentry, how to operate heavy equipment, and the tricks of road maintenance. He invited me to his house for coffee with his wife, treating me like the daughter they'd never had.

But Mark also had one of the park's least glamorous jobs: collecting and disposing of animal carcasses.

And somehow, I always ended up tagging along.

The first time, I didn't know what I was signing up for.

"Need a hand today?" I asked innocently.

Mark grinned. "Sure. Hop in the truck."

Twenty minutes later, we pulled up to a meadow where a buffalo had died. The smell hit me first—thick, unmistakable, impossible to ignore.

"Here," Mark said, handing me a small jar. "Vicks VapoRub. Dab some under your nose."

It helped. Barely.

We loaded the massive carcass into the dump truck bed—a process I won't describe in detail—and hauled it to a remote location where scavengers could do nature's cleanup safely away from tourists.

On the way back, we passed a tour bus. The guide was mid-speech when the tourists spotted us: a dump truck with a buffalo head flopping over the back.

The looks on their faces were priceless—confusion, horror, dawning realization.

That's not in the brochure.

Mark chuckled. "Never gets old."

"How often do we do this?" I asked.

"Often enough. Nature's messy. Part of the job."

After that, I always carried Vicks.

Law enforcement rangers also recruited me for projects—cutting hazardous trees, clearing rockslides, managing traffic during wildlife jams.

One ranger, Sarah, taught me chainsaw safety and the cardinal rule of bear country: never use power tools alone.

"Bears don't like loud noises," she said. "They'll usually avoid you. But surprise them—or get near cubs—and things can go sideways fast."

I took that rule seriously, especially after my first grizzly encounter.

I rounded a bend one morning and found myself face-to-face with a massive grizzly standing in the road.

We locked eyes.

Time stopped.

The bear huffed once, then ambled into the trees.

I sat frozen for a full minute before my hands stopped shaking enough to drive.

Welcome to Yellowstone.

Despite the hard work—and occasional terror, those first weeks were some of the happiest of my life.

Old Faithful became more than a tourist attraction on my third day off.

I stood among the crowd in jeans and a fleece jacket—just another visitor.

But I wasn't just another visitor.

When the geyser erupted, something inside me shifted. A quiet happiness settled in my chest, the kind that doesn't need words.

I'd made it.

From welfare lines to Yellowstone. From homelessness to purpose.

I thought of everything it took to get here.

And standing there, I realized:

This wasn't luck.

This was grace.

By late June, the park was buzzing with tourists, wildlife jams, and questions that tested my patience. But even on the hardest days, I never forgot how fortunate I was.

One evening, JoAnn and I watched the stars appear.

"You fit here," she said.

And for the first time in years, I believed it.

I had no idea what was coming next—but if Yellowstone had taught me anything, it was this:

The wild always has one more surprise waiting.

Between Destinations: Stories From My Journal Yellowstone

Here I Am!

On a brisk Friday morning, I bid farewell to Utah and embarked on a journey through Idaho, determined to reach Yellowstone before nightfall. As the miles rolled by, the mischievous whisper of adventure beckoned me toward a sign that read "Hot Springs." Surely, a soak would be the perfect end to a day of driving. I veered off the main route, only to find the hot springs were closed, a detour I could have done without.

With a sigh of frustration, I redirected my course through Jackson and the Grand Tetons, only to discover the southern gates of Yellowstone remained shut for the winter. This unexpected turn of events added another 4 to 5 hours to my trip and an additional tank of gas. I was weary and disheartened by the time I finally arrived at Yellowstone late Saturday afternoon. Although the landscape had been breathtaking, exhaustion dulled my appreciation of the stunning views.

The drive through the park seemed endless, taking me 18 miles beyond the edge of civilization to Tower Junction.

There, I arrived at the mobile home trailer that would be my new residence for the season. The cluster of accommodation included four two-bedroom trailers, three houses, and a bunkhouse.

Having endured cramped quarters the previous year, I was grateful for a trailer to

myself, yet the fatigue from the long drive overshadowed my excitement.

My new roommate, JoAnn, who was involved in the park's wolf project, greeted me warmly. I unpacked and set up my room, but the isolation and weariness left me feeling discontented. The nearest gas station was 80 miles south of Old Faithful, and the nearest town was 60 miles north, with another 30 miles to a larger town. Despite my best intentions to remain positive, I was disheartened by the realization that I'd missed an opportunity to mail some important documents.

Frustrated and questioning my decision, I took a few days to rest and acclimate. When I "finally drove out to the mail drop-off, a surprising discovery awaited me in Mammoth Springs: a charming town just 5 miles ahead. There, I found a gas station with prices that felt like a bargain, a well-stocked grocery store, and even a coffee house and bookstore. My spirits lifted as I realized I had access to everything I needed without having to travel far.

That evening, after a satisfying dinner and a newfound sense of contentment, JoAnn invited me for a walk. I agreed, expecting a leisurely stroll, but we soon found ourselves ascending a mountain trail leading to Lost Lake. JoAnn, equipped with bear spray, led the way, and I, reassured by her familiarity with the wilderness, followed. When she startled at the "first noise, I took the lead, guiding us safely back to camp.

Despite my huffing and puffing on the steep descent, the serene beauty of Lost Lake made the effort worthwhile.

JoAnn proposed we continue these evening hikes, and while I embraced the idea, I decided it was prudent to acquire my own can of bear spray. The rugged beauty of Yellowstone was beginning to win me over, but if a bear were to make me its meal, I wanted it on record that I never truly loved the park.

With a blend of apprehension and anticipation, I resolved to stay, ready to face the challenges.

and discoveries that lay ahead. Yellowstone, with all its wild charm and hidden surprises, was starting to feel like home.

Chapter 21
Learning the Ropes

By mid-July, I'd proven I could handle the basics. Vault toilets, trail maintenance, painting—all things I'd done variations of before, just in different settings.

Tom pulled me aside one morning after our crew meeting.

"You're doing good work, Spencer. Mark needs help with some carpentry work up at one of the ranger stations. You up for it?"

"Absolutely," I said.

"He mentioned you know your way around tools."

"Built plenty of furniture and did construction work back in California," I said. "I can hold my own."

Tom nodded. "Good. Report to him at seven-thirty tomorrow."

That's how I found myself in a pickup truck the next morning, tools rattling around as Mark drove up a winding mountain road to a remote ranger station that needed structural repairs.

"Tom says you've done framing before," Mark said as we unloaded supplies.

"Some. Residential construction in California. Plus, I built most of my furniture from scrap wood when I was on welfare. I'm better with a hammer than a nail gun, but I learn fast."

Mark grinned. "Fair enough. Let's see what you've got."

We worked side by side for hours. Mark handled the technical aspects—load-bearing calculations and building code requirements—while I fell into the familiar rhythm of measuring, cutting, and securing boards. My hands remembered the work, even if the setting was different.

"You weren't kidding," Mark said during lunch. "You know what you're doing."

"Years of practice," I said. "When you're raising three kids on welfare, you learn to fix everything yourself. Can't afford to call someone."

"Well, it shows." He took a bite of his sandwich. "Most seasonal workers can barely swing a hammer without hitting their thumb. But you? You move like you've been doing this your whole life."

"Not my whole life," I said. "But long enough."

After that, Mark became more of a colleague than a teacher. He explained park-specific requirements—why certain materials held up better in Yellowstone's extreme climate, which structures needed to withstand heavy snow loads—and I contributed what I knew about efficient building techniques and creative problem-solving.

"Where'd you learn to improvise like that?" he asked one afternoon after I jury-rigged a solution to a tricky corner joint.

"Farm in Utah," I said. "You learn to make do with what you have."

He laughed. "Sounds like you've lived a few different lives."

"Something like that."

The conversation shifted one day when Mark asked, "Are you thinking about coming back next season?"

I hadn't thought that far ahead. "Maybe. Why?"

"Because good workers are hard to find. People who show up on time, know their way around tools, and aren't afraid of hard work? Even harder. You'd be a fool not to come back."

That stayed with me. For so many years, I'd been told I wasn't enough—not educated enough, not skilled enough, not worthy enough. But here, someone valued what I could do.

It mattered.

Bear encounters continued, and my role slowly shifted from maintenance worker to de facto wildlife traffic controller.

The training video said ranger work was "rewarding and educational." It failed to mention you'd be asked the same questions seventy-three times a day:

"Where's the bathroom?"

"Is Old Faithful on a schedule?"

"Are the animals real?"

Yes, the animals are real. No, you can't pet the buffalo. Yes, that's a grizzly bear. No, I don't know what he's thinking. Probably you. As food.

Welcome to Yellowstone. I'm your ranger, and I'm as surprised to be here as you are.

One morning, I was assigned to manage an overlook where a black bear and her two cubs had taken up residence in a meadow.

Cars were stopped in the middle of the road, blocking traffic for miles.

My job was simple: keep people moving—and more importantly—keep them from doing something stupid.

"Ma'am, you need to stay in your vehicle," I said to a woman climbing out with a camera.

"But I want a better picture!"

"And that bear wants you to stay at least 100 yards away. Get back in your car."

She huffed but complied.

Five minutes later, someone else tried the same thing.

I'd dealt with difficult people before—welfare workers, landlords, ex-husbands—and tourists were no different. They just had better cameras.

"Sir, bears are dangerous. Vehicle. Now."

He started to argue.

"Now," I repeated, my voice flat and firm—the same tone I'd used a thousand times with my kids.

He got back in his car.

One afternoon, a man tried to hand-feed a bear cub.

I radioed for backup while running toward him. "Sir! Stop! Do NOT feed the bears!"

"It's just a baby," he said.

"And its mother is right over there," I replied, pointing to the massive sow now moving toward us.

The bear stood on her hind legs, huffed once, and started forward.

The man's face went white.

"Get in your car. NOW."

He practically teleported.

The ranger arrived moments later. Together, we cleared the area and closed the road.

"Good instincts," she said. "That could've gone very badly."

"I raised three kids," I said. "I know what a protective mother looks like."

She laughed. "Fair point."

In early August, my sister Louanne came to visit.

When I picked her up in my work truck, she was genuinely excited. We spent my days off sightseeing.

I worried she might judge the work—vault toilets weren't exactly glamorous—but when I explained that part of my day involved cleaning them, she grabbed gloves.

"I want to!" she said. "When else am I going to clean a toilet in Yellowstone National Park?"

We laughed through the work, turning the mundane into an adventure.

Louanne had an uncanny talent for attracting bears.

We'd hike a trail and suddenly—bear.

"Again?" I'd said.

"I can't help it!" she'd laugh.

One day, a black bear ambled straight toward us on a path. We bolted—leaping a fence and landing on my law enforcement neighbor's porch.

"Sorry!" I panted. "Bear!"

He lowered his weapon, watched the bear wander off, and shook his head. "You two are something else."

When Louanne left, she said, "Thanks for the fun vacation. I'll leave the bears here with you."

"Thanks for coming," I said. "It meant a lot."

As summer wore on, my responsibilities expanded—road construction, traffic control, painting, basic plumbing and electrical work.

Every paycheck, I saved what I could. Living in employee housing kept expenses low. The money grew slowly but steadily.

I didn't have a plan yet, but I wanted something permanent. Roots. A place of my own.

One weekend in late August, I wandered a hardware store in Bozeman, running my hands over lumber.

I wanted to build something.

A cabin.

But you can't build without land.

I thought of Utah. The farm. The affordability. Deanna.

I could do this.

By Labor Day, my decision was made.

On my last day, Tom pulled me aside.

"You did good work, Spencer. Real good. Planning to come back?"

"I think so," I said.

"We'll have you. Jobs post in February—call me."

Mark shook my hand. "Don't be a stranger."

JoAnn helped me pack. “It’s going to be quiet without you.”

“I’ll be back in the spring,” I promised.

Driving away from Yellowstone, I didn’t feel sad.

I felt ready.

Yellowstone reminded me I was capable of more than surviving.

Now it was time to thrive.

Between Destination: Stories From My Journal

Not Eaten by Bears Yet

Yes, I'm Still Here!

Could it be that the unrelenting weather is trying to keep me here on purpose? The days have been a relentless cycle of cold and rain, leaving me stranded indoors for what feels like forever. On my very first night in Yellowstone, the chill was so intense I wondered if my blankets were just decorative. Determined not to be a wimp, I resisted the urge to search for a thermostat. Miraculously, I made it through the night without turning into a human popsicle.

The next morning, my roommate sheepishly confessed that she had forgotten to turn the heat back on before bed—and had also left the kitchen window open. Suddenly, I didn't feel like such a wimp after all. I felt like a survivor.

As the weather slowly improved—though still moody, swinging between summer sunshine and arctic blast—I began to acclimate. On my first day of work, I joined a small but mighty team of eleven souls tucked away in this remote corner of the park. We had two law enforcement officers, my roommate, and about eight others from the maintenance department. Their warmth and friendliness were welcome comfort against the unpredictable cold.

My first assignment? Cleaning out the vault toilets. Not exactly the glamorous start I'd imagined. If there's a way to make an entrance, this probably wasn't it. Still, it gave me plenty of time to reflect on life choices and the importance of fresh air.

The rest of the day included paperwork, and later this week, I'll be helping with road work and flagging duties. It's a far cry from housekeeping, that's for sure.

My new abode is a cozy two-bedroom trailer. At first, I dreaded the thought of no running water. I'd grown accustomed to hauling buckets from a stream back home while remodeling—so I was ready to rough it again. But a quick check reminded me that here, the water runs when you turn the handle. That alone felt like a luxury vacation.

So yes, I'm still here — adjusting, laughing, and, most importantly, not eaten by any bears yet.

Chapter 22
A Piece of Earth

I left for Yellowstone in May 2004 feeling broken and desperate. I came back to Utah in October feeling capable and strong. Yellowstone had done that—given me confidence, taught me new skills, and reminded me I could do hard things.

While I was gone, Deanna had made a big change of her own. She'd left the farm and bought a fixer-upper across town. All summer, she'd written to me about it, sent updates, even left directions. When I pulled into Utah, I drove straight there and moved in to help.

"Welcome home! How was it?" she asked, handing me a hammer and pointing at a wall.

"Amazing," I said. "Exhausting. Amazing."

We jumped straight into the remodel. The place needed everything—walls repaired, floors redone, windows replaced. It felt good to build again, to hear the steady rhythm of a hammer and smell fresh-cut wood.

Mom was visiting that weekend, so the three of us sat around the kitchen table that night while I told stories—the tourists, the bears, Mark's mentorship, Louanne's visit. They laughed and listened like they were right there in Yellowstone with me.

"So, you're going back in the spring?" Deanna asked, tapping a blueprint.

"Definitely. But I need winter work. Glad you hired me," I teased. "I can't sit still for six months."

Winter was coming, and for the first time in a long time, I didn't have a solid plan. That should've scared me—but it didn't. Something inside me had been taking shape all summer.

"I'm buying that land," I said suddenly.

Deanna looked up from loading the wood stove. "The lot across the street?"

"Yes. I'm going to build a cabin. Something permanent. My own place."

She broke into a grin. "It's available, and it's perfect! We can help each other out—you with your cabin, me with this place. This is going to be fun."

Saying it out loud made it real. I was finally going to own a piece of earth.

The acre was covered in thick sagebrush—tall, tangled, untouched. The scent of dry sage clung to everything, brushing my arms as I walked through it. Instead of an overgrown lot, I saw a foundation. A porch facing the mountains. A small cabin with a warm light in the window.

"How much?" I asked the owner.

He quoted a price far higher than I'd saved. My stomach sank.

"Could we do a payment plan?" I asked.

After a long pause, he nodded. "Put down what you've got, and we'll figure out the rest. Better someone use it than let it sit."

"Deal," I said before he could change his mind.

Two weeks later, I signed the papers. One acre. Mine.

That afternoon, I stood in the brisk wind, sagebrush brushing my boots, and quietly said, "I own this." After years of moving, renting, living in shelters and borrowed rooms, I finally owned something solid.

Deanna was thrilled. "We're going to be neighbors!"

That night, I stood on the property again under a sky thick with stars. The mountains were dark silhouettes. The air smelled like pine and earth.

"Thank you," I whispered—to God, the universe, whatever had carried me from welfare lines to this moment.

But there was one problem.

The sagebrush.

Before I could build anything, the land had to be cleared—and this stuff grew like it had a personal grudge. I tried digging. The roots were two feet deep, and the brush towered over me. My hands blistered. My arms burned.

"This is going to take forever," I muttered.

Deanna had a solution. "Bring the horses over."

"The horses?" I blinked.

"Let them loose. They'll trample the sagebrush. It's how we cleared part of our pasture."

I was skeptical, but desperate. We fenced off the acre and brought the horses over.

For weeks, they treated my land like a personal playground—running, stomping, munching, kicking up dust. They were furry bulldozers with hooves. And it worked. Slowly, the sagebrush flattened. The roots broke apart. Bare ground started to appear.

As space opened up, I imagined the cabin—where the windows would go, where the porch would face, what sunrise would look like from my doorstep.

"I'll work Yellowstone again," I told Deanna. "Save money for materials. Start the walls next fall."

It was a long-term plan, maybe two years until it was finished. But I had time. And for the first time in my adult life, I had a dream that was mine.

Winter arrived hard. Snow covered everything, hiding the horses' progress. I took a temporary job in town, saving every dollar. On weekends, I stood on the snow-covered acre, notebook in hand, sketching ideas: a 400-square-foot cabin, a sleeping loft, a wood stove. Simple. Strong. Mine.

Mom visited in February, and I brought her to see it.

"Once the snow melts, you'll see what the horses cleared," I said.

We stood there—two women who'd survived more than most people knew—looking at an empty lot and seeing a future.

Spring crept in slowly. The snow melted, revealing the flattened sagebrush. Still rough. Still wild. But finally workable.

In early March, I called Yellowstone and confirmed I was returning for the 2005 season.

This time, I wasn't going back searching for myself. This time, I had a mission: save every penny and come home ready to build.

The day before I left, I stood on the property one more time. The land looked better now—tamed enough to imagine a cabin sitting right in the center.

Home.

"I'll be back," I told the empty acre. "And when I come back, we're building something."

I climbed into my truck, pointed it north toward Wyoming, and smiled.

This wasn't just the beginning of another season.

It was the beginning of building a life—literally, with my own two hands.

I headed back to Yellowstone thinking everything was finally lining up. But if life has taught me anything, it's this: the minute you start feeling confident, the universe whispers, Oh really? Watch this.

Between Destination: Stories From My Journal

Toto, We're Not in Kansas Anymore! (Or Utah for That Matter)

Arriving in Yellowstone in early April was like stepping into another world — one where winter had clearly decided it wasn't done yet. Most of the roads were still closed, except for the northeast highway that skirts the Montana border.

The year before, I'd arrived later in the season and missed the early season "fun." This year was different. After the long drive to West Yellowstone, I was low on funds and patience, only to be redirected all the way to Bozeman, Montana, because the park's West entrance was still shut — with no clear opening date. It was as if Yellowstone was saying, "Welcome back… sort of."

Once I started work, I realized I was among the very few early arrivals. Weekends were so quiet, I could practically hear the snow melt. The housing area was deserted, the kind of silence where even your thoughts start to echo. During the week, only a handful of us were around, and for two weekends straight, I was entirely alone — thirty miles from the nearest human being.

At first, the solitude didn't bother me.

I stayed indoors at night, watching all the videos I'd brought (some of them twice), reading books and magazines, writing letters, and taking short walks. But as the weeks wore on, the isolation began to gnaw at me. I was warned to be extra cautious around bears since they were just coming out of hibernation — hungry, cranky, and not interested in small talk.

I saw at least two bears on my work route, along with other wildlife, which didn't exactly put me at ease.

One day, while driving through one of my favorite walking areas, I rounded a corner and came face-to-face with a bear. We made eye contact — me frozen behind the wheel, the bear looking unimpressed — and I decided right then that discretion was the better part of valor. That trail was officially closed… permanently… at least to me.

After that, I holed up inside, rewatching my videos until I could quote the dialogue, reread my magazines, and building shelves out of scrap wood. I cleaned my already spotless quarters, wrote more letters, and finished every book I owned.

Eventually, boredom pushed me to try again. I ventured outside one weekend for a walk — only to be greeted by a cinnamon bear standing at the bottom of the steps.

"Okay," I thought. "You win."

I locked the door and decided to be productive indoors. When cabin fever struck again, I tried the back door — only to find myself face-to-face with a massive buffalo.

We stared at each other for a moment, neither one of us blinking. Then he grunted, snot dripping from his nose, and stomped his foot.

I decided he could have the yard.

Back inside I went — re-cleaning everything, re-rereading my magazines, and mentally preparing myself for a future career in indoor living.

But determination (or maybe stubbornness) kicked in again. I put on my shoes and tried the front door. And there, waiting for me, was a black bear.

That was it. Three doors, three animals. Clearly, I was under some kind of wildlife house arrest.

Then I had an idea.

The next morning, I woke up early — before the animals knew I was awake — and sneaked out like a fugitive. I was good. I outsmarted them. I made it all the way to Bozeman for an all-day outing, window-shopping and mentally cataloging everything I'd buy once I had money: a loaf of bread, colorful candles, maybe a new lock for my doors.

When I returned to the bunkhouse, I looked out the window to see the animals, one by one, circling my truck, sniffing the bumper, and probably wondering how I'd escaped.

Finally, when summer arrived, the animals retreated to higher ground, and the park filled with employees and tourists. No longer under the watchful eyes of my animal "guards," I could finally breathe easy.

But as I watched the bears and other wildlife now cornered by cars, cameras, and crowds, I couldn't help but feel that the tables had turned.

Now they were the ones under house arrest.

Another season in Yellowstone had begun — and I had officially learned that in the battle between humans and nature, the bears always win.

Chapter 23
Ranger by Day, Carpenter by Night

The drive to Yellowstone in late April felt different than the year before. Back then, I'd been nervous and unsure; this time, I knew exactly what I was walking into—and I was ready. My truck held the same old camping supplies and canned goods, but now there was something new tucked inside: a notebook filled with cabin sketches, material lists, and measurements. Every spare moment that summer would go toward planning, calculating, and saving.

I had a mission now.

The park was still locked in winter when I arrived—snow piled high along the roads, ice clinging to the trees, and only a handful of employees moving with the practiced efficiency of people who knew exactly what they were doing.

I was one of them now.

Tom greeted me at the maintenance office with a nod.

"Spencer. Good to see you back."

"Good to be back," I said.

"You're in the bunkhouse this year—alone for the first few months." He handed me a key. "We've got a lot of early prep—roads to clear, facilities to check. You up for it?"

"Absolutely."

JoAnn welcomed me with her usual burst of enthusiasm. "You came back! I wasn't sure you would."

"How was your winter?" she asked.

"Busy," I said. "I bought land. I'm building a cabin."

Her jaw dropped. "You're doing it yourself?"

"That's the plan. The foundation is already laid. This summer's paychecks will buy the framing materials."

She flipped through my sketches, impressed. "Ambitious. But knowing you? You'll do it."

Mark was already in the shop the next morning, coffee in hand.

"Spencer," he said with a rare smile. "Heard you're back."

"Couldn't stay away."

"Tom says you're not starting with vault toilets this year."

"Thank God."

"You've graduated," he said. "Carpentry crew—full time. Some road work too."

Carpentry crew. Not cleaning. Skilled work. I'd earned it.

The early season was brutal but beautiful. Tom and Mark were assigned to another part of the park for the first few months, so I handled the shop and roads alone. With most of the park still closed, it felt like working inside a cathedral—quiet, raw, sacred. Bears stumbled out of hibernation. Bison owned the roads. Wolves howled at dawn.

My days fell into a rhythm: up before sunrise, grab coffee, attack whatever project needed attention.

Painting, repairs, fence rebuilds, new storage structures. Every swing of the hammer made me stronger. Every paycheck went straight into the cabin fund.

On days off, I didn't explore like I had the year before. Instead, I sat on the bunkhouse steps with my notebook, refining measurements, calculating costs, and buying small tools in town. Part of me stayed in Utah—standing on that acre of land, imagining walls rising from the foundation.

Tourists arrived in June, and chaos came with them. Traffic jams, bear jams, geyser crowds, and the same questions repeated like a script:

"When do you turn on the geysers?"

"Are the animals real?"

"Can I pet that bison?"

(You can—but you'll regret it.)

One afternoon, I was assigned to traffic control near a mama grizzly and her two cubs.

"Ma'am, stay in your vehicle."

"But I just want one picture."

"That bear weighs four hundred pounds and can run thirty-five miles an hour. You want that picture bad enough to bet your life on it?"

She got back into her car. Five minutes later, someone else tried the exact same thing. That job required the patience of a saint.

Still, there were quiet moments—early mornings before the crowds and late evenings after they left—that reminded me why I loved this place.

That summer, Mark and I rebuilt the firehouse garage.

"This is historic preservation," he said. "Everything must match the original construction."

We worked side by side for weeks, barely talking—just measuring, cutting, fitting, nailing. The rhythm was meditative.

One afternoon, he asked, "You planning to come back next year?"

"I don't know. I've got a cabin to build. Winter hits hard in Utah—I need walls up before snow."

He nodded. "Makes sense. You've got good instincts. Shame to lose you."

"Maybe I'll come back after the cabin's done."

"Maybe," he said.

But we both knew I probably wouldn't.

By late August, I wasn't counting down because I wanted to leave—I was counting down because I had work waiting at home. Real work. My cabin.

Every paycheck had been earmarked: lumber, roofing, windows. The foundation was already laid. That winter, framing would begin.

During my last week, Tom pulled me aside.

"You're planning on coming back next year?"

"Probably not," I said. "I've got a cabin to build."

He nodded. "Figured. You've done solid work here, Spencer. Two good seasons."

"Thanks, Tom."

"Well," he said, extending his hand, "go build something."

"That's the plan."

My last day was bittersweet. I said goodbye to JoAnn, shook hands with the crew, and Mark walked me to my truck.

"You learned well," he said.

"Thanks for everything," I replied.

"You did the work," he said simply. "I just pointed you in the right direction."

As I drove away that September afternoon, I didn't look back—not because I didn't love the place, but because what waited ahead mattered more.

I'd saved aggressively—enough for framing lumber, windows, and roofing. Not everything, but enough to make real progress.

The drive back to Utah felt shorter than ever. I was eager, energized, ready to swing a hammer and watch walls rise from the foundation.

Deanna was waiting when I pulled up.

"Ready to build?"

"Let's do this."

And we did.

The sun beat down on us, the smell of sawdust mixing with the earthy scent of trampled sagebrush. Hot, dusty, sweaty work—but we thrived in it, laughing as we worked toward something that finally felt real.

I thought the hardest part was behind me—hauling lumber, pounding nails, wrestling sagebrush.

But building would prove me wrong.

Turns out, the real challenges were just getting started.

Between Destination: Stories From My Journal
Just for Laughs

Living in isolation in Yellowstone has its perks, but keeping myself entertained was sometimes a challenge. After exhausting my collection of books, magazines, and DVDs (to the point where I could recite entire scenes from memory), I had to get a bit creative to stave off boredom.

During the day, I kept busy with work, hiking, and the occasional field trip. But as dusk fell and the wildlife emerged for their evening snacks, I knew better than to risk becoming part of the food chain. So, most evenings, I stayed inside. With the park still quiet before the main tourist season, those nights felt particularly still.

Without Wi-Fi in my housing unit, my entertainment options were limited. We had a communal computer in the office next door, available for all employees. One evening, after aimlessly scrolling online, I decided it was time to try something new. That's when I stumbled upon a dating site. Why not? I thought. Maybe I'll find a local resident to hang out with.

Feeling adventurous, I put together a decent profile and hit submit.

On my next day off, I headed back to the computer, curious to see if there were any matches.

To my surprise, I had a hit—from a local in Mammoth Hot Springs!

My heart raced with excitement and nerves as I clicked to see who it might be. Could it be a new friend—or maybe something more?

With bated breath, I clicked the link. And there it was—my own profile staring back at me!

I couldn't help but burst out laughing. Somehow, I had managed to match myself. Note to self: I'm not the most tech-savvy person, and perhaps I shouldn't be left alone with a computer for too long. At least I succeeded in entertaining myself in the most unexpected way!

Chapter 24
Crossroads of Destiny: Choices and Consequence

By late October 2005, the Utah cold was already setting in, and winter work was essential. That's when I saw it: seasonal positions at a Colorado ski resort. Good pay. Employee housing included. Perfect timing—work November through March, then head back to Yellowstone for another summer season.

It made sense financially. More than that, it made sense strategically. Earn money all winter, return to Utah in spring with enough saved to buy more materials, then work in Yellowstone all summer. By fall, I would be ready to make serious progress on the cabin.

I called and landed an interview. They loved my maintenance experience and offered me a position on the spot, starting in late November.

When I told Mom about my plan, she tilted her head and said, "Oh… that's good. I'm glad you got a job out there."

Mom had moved back from the Grand Canyon in June, parking her travel trailer on Deanna's property. Her old hip injury had worsened, making the physical demands of her job there too difficult.

"Just glad?" I asked, raising an eyebrow.

She shrugged with that half-smile that always meant trouble. "Well… you know me. Winter in Utah isn't exactly retirement paradise. My hip aches. The propane bills could probably fund a small country. And groceries?" She sighed. "Let's just say I've become very good at soup."

"You know, you could come with me," I said. "The ski resort is hiring for all kinds of positions—cafeteria, gift shop, housekeeping. Employee housing included. We'd both have steady income through the winter."

Mom waved her hand dismissively. "Me? Oh no, no. I'll be fine here. Really. You go do your thing."

"You sure?"

"Absolutely. I'm fine."

The next morning, I went out to load my truck and stopped dead.

Every single one of Mom's suitcases was already packed in the back.

I stared at them, then walked back inside. "Mom?"

She peeked around the corner, looking entirely too innocent.

"What happened to 'I'll be fine here'?" I asked.

She shrugged. "Well… I got to thinking. You're going to need supervision. Someone to make sure you don't get frostbite—or build that cabin crooked."

"So, you packed. In the middle of the night."

"It was early morning, technically."

I couldn't help it, I laughed. This was classic Mom. Never admit you want something directly. Just pack your bags and pretend it was a practical necessity.

"Okay," I said. "Let's go."

I made the calls, sent in her application, and soon she had an interview scheduled. Before long, we were both hired.

November was cold and clear. Mom and I loaded up the car and headed to Colorado, optimistic about the winter ahead. We would work, save money, and return in spring ready to tackle the next phase of construction.

That was the plan.

When we arrived in Colorado, the ski resort wasn't quite ready for us.

"Personnel delays," they explained. "Your start date is pushed back a week. Maybe two. We'll let you know."

We managed to get temporary mailboxes in town and stayed in Leadville while we waited for housing to open up. But as storms rolled in and travel became impossible, two weeks turned into three. Three turned into four.

We were already committed—given up our housing in Utah, driven all this way, spent what little money we had. We were stuck in limbo, burning through savings while waiting for either the jobs to start or the storms to clear.

Neither happened.

The weeks dragged on, savings dwindled, and we ended up at a hostel, trying to stretch what little money we had.

Then another major snowstorm rolled in—the kind of blizzard that shuts down entire regions.

And then Mom got sick.

It started with fatigue and nausea, then worsened. A doctor diagnosed her with a severe illness, likely a flu complication, though they couldn't pinpoint the source. She was put on medication and ordered to rest.

Rest. In a hostel. Waiting for jobs that might never materialize.

We had almost no money left. Mom was too weak to travel. Winter was closing in fast.

That's when someone told us about the women's shelter.

I'd been homeless before. I lived in shelters with my kids. I knew what to expect. But this felt different.

This felt like failure.

I'd worked so hard to escape that life. I'd built skills, saved money, and bought land. I was literally building my own home.

And now I was back in a shelter—sleeping in a bunk bed, following rules about when I could come and go.

But we had no choice.

The shelter took us in just as the blizzard hit. Snow fell for days, shutting down roads and trapping us there. Mom wasn't strong enough to travel anyway. She spent most of her time resting while I tried to figure out our next move.

The shelter had strict rules: out by 8 a.m., back by 5 p.m.

We spent our days staying warm wherever we could. Home Depot's café became our morning routine—terrible coffee, but it was hot and free. Target for window shopping. Safeway during their grand opening, packed with free samples.

The library became our refuge—warm, quiet, with internet access and a café. We blended in with other patrons; you couldn't tell who was from the shelter and who wasn't. Whole Foods offered free samples that sometimes doubled as lunch. On St. Patrick's Day, we scored corned beef meals for a few dollars—a feast by our standards.

God always seemed to provide exactly what we needed, exactly when we needed it.

As weeks turned into months, reality set in: the ski resort jobs weren't coming. Start dates were pushed back again and again—excuses, promises, nothing solid.

We were trapped.

Four months.

We spent four months in that shelter.

Living there together forced Mom and me to depend on each other in ways we never had before. She'd been absent for much of my life. Now she was my roommate, my companion, my responsibility.

Something shifted—not dramatically, not emotionally. Just proximity. Day after day together.

She'd always known about my welfare years. But knowing about hardships and living it are different things.

Now she understood what I'd endured—the humiliation, exhaustion, and the constant fight to survive with dignity intact.

We didn't talk about the past. We didn't fix anything.

We survived together.

One cold morning, sitting in the Home Depot café, Mom said, "This coffee tastes like dirt."

"Yep," I said.

"But it's warm."

"Yep."

That was the extent of our bonding.

Some relationships don't get fixed. They just get… tolerated.

And sometimes, that's enough.

When the roads finally cleared in late March and Mom was strong enough to travel, we had a decision to make.

We didn't return to Utah. We didn't go back to the cabin.

That hurt more than I wanted to admit. I'd laid the foundation. Cleared the land. Spent two summers saving every penny.

But I had no money left. Mom needed stability. And Yellowstone was the only sure thing I had.

The cabin would have to wait.

We packed what little we had and pointed the car north—toward Wyoming, toward Yellowstone, toward another season in the mountains where I already had a job offer waiting.

Mom was practical. "I'm not going back to Utah. Too cold. Too isolated. I need somewhere I can afford."

"What about near Yellowstone?" I asked. "You could look for housing while I work."

She considered it. "That could work."

"Okay," I said. "Let's go north."

So that's what we did.

The cabin would have to wait.

Those four months in the shelter didn't fix our relationship. Mom was still Mom—practical, distant, allergic to emotional conversations.

But we survived together.

Not everything.

But something.

As we headed north toward Yellowstone, the ache of leaving the cabin behind settled deep in my chest. I told myself it was temporary.

But life has a way of rearranging plans.

And what waited in Yellowstone that spring was nothing like I expected.

Not even close.

Between Destination: Stories From My Journal

Two Roads Diverged in the Woods

"Two roads diverged in the woods, and I took the one less traveled, and it made all the difference in the world." —Robert Frost

As I sit atop my bunk, the world around me fades, and the music from my Walkman transports me to another place. I bought this little device at a store, hoping it would help keep my thoughts in check. Earlier today, frustration bubbled over — not just with the people around me, but with myself. I'd been bottling up emotions for too long, and with no outlet left, I turned to my music.

This winter has been brutal — the coldest this town has seen in years. I feel lost, caught between the life I had and whatever lies ahead. The shelter, once filled with familiar faces, has grown quiet. Almost everyone I knew had moved on, leaving just a few of us behind.

Living in a homeless shelter is an experience like no other. From my top bunk, I look out over rows of empty beds — fourteen in total, twenty-eight when you count both levels. I always get the top bunk because you need a doctor's note to sleep on the bottom.

Normally, I wouldn't mind, but these beds are like oversized cribs — you must climb over rails to get out. Most mornings, I find fresh bruises on my legs from the effort.

The room has grown eerily silent this week.

Beside me lies "Rooster," a woman whose nickname stuck long before I arrived. Her real name is Jane. She's been here longer than anyone I know. Her dyed blonde hair has long since surrendered to dark roots, and she rarely combs it or makes her bed — just crawls in and out, always wearing her jacket, as if she's ready to run but nowhere to go.

Like all of us, she has a story. Some of us are well-dressed, others not. Some are fighting to rebuild; others are trying to make it through another day. But all of us — every single one — have ended up here after taking the road less traveled.

If I were rich, I wouldn't spend my time and money in other countries. I'd start here, in America. I'd buy sleeping bags and pads for those still out in the cold — the ones who don't even have a top bunk to climb into.

The shelter rules are strict but fair. No sharp objects. No drugs. No alcohol. We're out by 8:00 a.m. and can't return until 5:00 p.m. Dinner's at 6:00. These hours are generous compared to other shelters. Meals are served on metal trays, eaten side by side in the dining room. If you're not in line for breakfast by 6:30 a.m., you miss it — and the coffee pot's usually empty by 6:14.

Volunteers serve our meals — college students looking for extra credit, middle-class folks wanting to "give back," church groups trying to do their part. They probably think they're doing us a favor, but I sometimes think it's the other way around. We're giving them a glimpse of real life — the kind you can't find in textbooks or sermons.

After dinner, it is shower time and then lights out. The lights shut off automatically at 10:00 p.m. and flicker back on at 6:00 a.m. If you want to sleep early, you learn to do it with a blanket over your head. Some of us go to work; most of us spend the day on the streets.

When I go to the library, I see familiar faces — people sitting on benches or at computers, trying to look busy. We all share the same secret: we're homeless. But no one knows our stories.

Every morning, I wake up determined to make a change. And every night, I return defeated. I was only supposed to stay here for a few days — but days turned into weeks. My future feels as fragile as a wilting flower under summer heat, thirsty for relief that never comes.

"Two roads diverged in the woods, and I took the one less traveled, and it made all the difference in the world." —Robert Frost

I've been the Good Samaritan — rescuing a family member from their own storm, putting my life on hold, and sleeping among strangers. I've made friends with the unknown, cried in the dark, and laughed in the daylight.

I'm still determined to make a difference.

But some nights, when the music fades and the world is still, I can't help but wonder — what if I had taken the other road?

Chapter 25

Pit Stops, Promises, and False Hope

Arriving at Yellowstone in April 2006 felt like coming home—but also like visiting a place I'd already outgrown.

The snow was melting, revealing muddy trails and soggy meadows. The maintenance crew greeted me like an old friend. Tom handed me my key and assignment sheet without preamble.

"Spencer. Welcome back. Same deal as last year—you're on the carpentry crew. Mark's already here."

"Good to be back," I said. And I meant it. Sort of.

Mom came with me this time, determined to find her own housing nearby. I dropped her off at a motel in a nearby town while she started making calls, checking bulletin boards, and asking around.

"I'll find something," she said confidently. "You go to work."

Within a week, she'd secured a small rental house about an hour and a half from the park. Not close, but close enough for weekend visits. She seemed content with the arrangement—her own space, her independence, but family nearby if needed.

It worked for both of us.

My third season at Yellowstone was different from the start.

I wasn't learning anymore. I was executing. Tom and Mark trusted me with complex projects, sent me out solo to handle repairs, and asked my opinion on construction decisions.

"What do you think, Spencer?" Mark would ask.

And I'd give him an answer that made sense—because I knew what I was doing now.

The work was satisfying, but something had shifted. Every nail I hammered, every board I cut, every project I completed—my mind was elsewhere.

In Utah. On my property.

Where walls were waiting to be raised, where a roof needed to go, where a cabin was half-built and calling me home.

I'd wake up in the bunkhouse thinking, I wish I could be working on my cabin right now.

The restlessness was constant now. Not occasional daydreams—full-blown, can't-ignore-it restlessness. I'd explored every trail, every geyser, every hidden corner of Yellowstone. The park was breathtaking, awe-inspiring, and full of challenges—but I'd seen it all.

The crowds, the congested roads, the endless stream of tourists—it wore on me. Even the isolation I'd once craved had become routine, predictable, and a little stifling. I needed something else. Something new.

I wanted work that felt different—a place where I could build something tangible and see the results of my effort.

Yellowstone had taught me I could do hard things. But now I was ready for a challenge that was mine alone to shape.

That summer, after settling back into life at Yellowstone, I made plans to head to Colorado to retrieve my truck, the one I'd purchased the previous winter but hadn't yet picked up. Airfare didn't fit my schedule or budget, so I decided to take the Greyhound bus.

It wasn't glamorous, but it was practical.

Besides, I told myself, how bad could it be?

Mom dropped me off at the station, and my son Jacob agreed to meet me for dinner in Denver once I arrived. He'd moved the truck into storage for safekeeping, and we were both looking forward to catching up.

At first, the trip went smoothly. We rolled through Montana, passed Billings, and crossed into Wyoming without a hitch.

Then things started to unravel.

The bus began overheating—repeatedly. Each time the driver pulled over, he'd announce, "We'll let it cool down. Stretch your legs if you want."

Out we'd go, standing on the shoulder of the freeway while cars and semis thundered past. There wasn't much to look at—just endless grass, sagebrush, and the occasional bewildered cow watching our roadside parade.

At first, the unscheduled stops were almost funny. Passengers joked about Greyhound's new "scenic detour package." But after the fifth or sixth breakdown, the humor evaporated.

Each time, we were told a replacement bus was coming. Each time, it wasn't.

The driver would tinker under the hood, fire up the engine, and we'd limp another few miles—only to repeat the whole ritual. The day stretched into evening, and everyone's patience wore thin.

By the time we reached Colorado, I knew my dinner plans with Jacob were doomed. I'd been updating him throughout the journey, but after the fourth delay, he texted, Are you ever getting here?

As fate would have it, the bus overheated again right outside Longmont—Jacob's town. We coasted to a stop on the shoulder of the freeway, barely a block from his exit.

That was it.

I grabbed my backpack and told the woman beside me, "I'm done. I'm getting off here."

She stared at me like I'd lost my mind. Maybe I had—but I wasn't spending another hour stranded on that bus.

I climbed down, stood there for a moment, and watched the bus rumble away, leaving me alone beside the freeway with my backpack and stubborn determination.

I called Jacob.

"Where are you?" he asked.

"On the freeway near your off-ramp."

"The freeway?" he said. "You mean the bus station?"

"No," I said, trying not to laugh. "The freeway. I got off. Can you come get me?"

There was a pause long enough to make me wonder if he'd hung up.

"You got off the bus?" he said.

"Yes."

"On the freeway?"

"Yes, Jacob. I'm literally standing next to the freeway. Cars are flying by. I'm waving at semis."

"You can't get off a bus on the freeway!"

"Well, apparently, I can. Because I did."

Fifteen minutes later, Jacob pulled up, shaking his head and laughing so hard he could barely park.

"Mom," he said, "only you would do this."

Later, he told me what happened when his coworkers asked where he was going.

"I'm picking up my mom," he said.

"Oh, from the airport?"

"No."

"The bus station?"

"Nope."

They blinked. "Then where?"

"From the freeway."

The looks on their faces were priceless.

It could've been a miserable trip—but instead, it became one of those stories you tell for years, the kind that turns inconvenient into laughter.

After a warm visit with my kids and a few real meals, I retrieved my truck and headed back to Yellowstone. The open road felt familiar: endless sky, pine air, and a sense of freedom that revived me.

Knowing it would be my last summer in Yellowstone, I soaked in every view, every quiet sunrise, every moment of gratitude.

Because the journey had taught me this:

The best stories often come from detours you never planned.

My last day at Yellowstone came in early September 2006.

I packed the bunkhouse, loaded my truck, and said goodbye. JoAnn made me promise—again—to send pictures of the finished cabin. Mark walked me out one last time.

"Good luck," he said.

"Thanks for everything."

As I drove away, I didn't feel sad.

I felt complete.

Yellowstone had given me exactly what I needed—skills, confidence, income, and proof that I could do hard things. But it had always been a steppingstone, not a destination.

Now it was time to step forward.

I drove straight to Utah, where Deanna was waiting.

"Ready to finish this cabin?" she asked.

"Let's do it."

And over the next two years—working winters and summers, saving from odd jobs, learning as I went, I did exactly that.

I built my cabin.

With my own two hands.

Every board. Every nail. Every decision.

It wasn't perfect.

It was mine.

And that made all the difference.

Chapter 26
Breaking Boundaries
Freed in the Wild

When I pulled into Deanna's driveway that September afternoon in 2006, the first thing I did was walk across the street to my property.

The foundation waited for me exactly as I'd left it nearly a year earlier. The partial framing stood bare against the sky—weathered, but solid. Around it, the land held the marks of our early work: flattened sagebrush, cleared patches, the promise of something real.

I stood there, hands on my hips, mentally calculating everything that needed to happen next.

Roof. Windows. Doors. Walls insulated and sealed. Interior framing. Electrical. Maybe plumbing, if I could swing it. Wood stove installation.

It was overwhelming.

It was also exactly what I wanted to be doing.

Deanna stepped up beside me. "So, what's first?"

"Roof," I said without hesitation. "Winter's coming. If I can get a roof on before snow hits, I can work inside all winter."

"When do we start?"

I grinned. "Tomorrow."

Building a Dream, One Board at a Time.

The next two years became a blur of sawdust, lumber, and determination.

I took whatever odd jobs I could find—temporary maintenance, short contracts, anything that paid. When I had money, I bought materials. When I had materials, I built. When winter made outside work impossible, I moved inside to frame, plan, measure, and prepare.

The cabin rose slowly, stubbornly, one board at a time.

Deanna helped whenever she could—holding boards while I nailed, running to town for supplies, offering another pair of steady hands. We fell into a rhythm: work until we couldn't anymore, break for a bite, then get right back at it.

Some days we worked until dark, our breath turning white in the cold, determined to finish just one more section.

The roof went up that first fall. Deanna had learned roofing skills working with a friend in town, and she climbed places I had no desire to climb. I handed her tools from the ground—sometimes even sent lunch up to her.

When we finally stood back and looked at the finished roof, Utah mountains behind us, I felt something profound:

I'm really doing this.

Winter Comes Hard

Winter hit fast that year.

Snow covered the property, but now I have a roof overhead.

I worked inside, installing tongue-and-groove on the ceiling, measuring for windows, planning the loft that would be my bedroom.

I bought a small generator. Added a few tiny appliances. Worked in layers of clothing. My breath still puffed white in the air, but at least my hands worked. On the coldest days, I retreated to Deanna's house to sketch plans and order supplies.

Money was tighter than it had ever been at Yellowstone. Every purchase had to be justified. Every board counted. I learned to scavenge, repurpose, and make do.

A neighbor donated an old RV, nothing fancy, but perfect for storage.

Deanna and I salvaged lumber from the dump when allowed.

A construction site tossed perfectly usable 2x4s with minor warping; I hauled home everyone I could find.

It wasn't glamorous.

But it worked.

God provided—through generosity, resourcefulness, and the sheer stubbornness that kept me building even on the hardest days.

By spring 2007, the walls were up and insulated. Windows installed. The door—a solid, beautiful door I built from clearance wood at Home Depot.

I even splurged on tile behind the wood stove. Some things were worth doing right.

Standing inside those four walls, surrounded by the smell of fresh pine and sawdust, I felt deep pride.

This was mine.

I'd built this.

Not hired it out.

Not inherited it.

Built it—with my own hands, with every skill I'd picked up in Yellowstone, every hard job I'd ever done, every setback I'd clawed my way through.

One Season Away, Then Back Again

That next winter, I took a short-term maintenance contract at Mount Rushmore. The pay was good—good enough to carry me through another summer of building. Good enough to finally hire a tractor to plow the land properly.

When I returned to Utah that spring, I had enough saved to buy the interior tongue-and-groove paneling I'd dreamed about. Installing it was meditative:

Measure, cut, fit, nail.

Measure, cut, fit, nail.

Piece by piece, the cabin took shape.

Deanna helped when she could. I helped remodel her house in return. We stayed busy, as always. We also spent long days in the high country cutting permitted trees and hauling them home for firewood.

The work never really ended.

The wood stove installation was my biggest challenge. I cut a hole through the roof myself, installed flashing, built a rock hearth from salvaged stone, and maneuvered the heavy cast-iron stove I'd bought in South Dakota.

When I lit that first fire and the smoke flowed perfectly, I wanted to shout for joy.

That stove warmed my first night in the cabin—and every night that followed.

The Loft, the Light, the Life I Built.

The loft became my favorite part—framed by hand, ladder-accessed, just big enough for a bed and dresser. From up there, I could see the whole cabin.

Small, yes.

But perfect.

Every inch was intentional.

Every window placed for the best light.

Every nook measured for storage.

Every beam chosen with purpose.

This wasn't just shelter.

This was home.

By 2008, the Dream Was Real

By winter 2008, the cabin was nearly complete.

Interior walls done.

Loft functional.

Wood stove warm even on the coldest nights.

Basic electrical installed—with help from a licensed electrician for the tricky parts.

Plumbing could wait. I had what I needed.

I moved in before it was technically finished. I couldn't wait any longer.

That first night in my own loft, listening to the wind whistle past walls I had built, I barely slept.

Not from discomfort—but from joy.

I had done it.

Home, Finished

Deanna came over the next morning with coffee and breakfast.

"How was your first night?" she asked.

"Perfect," I said. "Absolutely perfect."

We sat on the floor—no furniture yet—drinking coffee and studying the space where future memories would live.

"Thanks for helping," I said. "I couldn't have done this without you."

The finishing touches came slowly.

Trim.

Shelves.

Counter space.

Hooks.

A little table made from scrap wood.

Jacob and Heidi had come to visit They toured the cabin with wide eyes, climbing the loft ladder, touching walls, asking how I'd done this or that.

"This is amazing, Mom," Jacob said.

"It's not fancy," I told him. "But it's mine."

"It's better than fancy," he said. "It's real."

By late fall 2008, the cabin was fully livable. Imperfect, sure—but whole. Mine.

I stood on the small porch I'd built, staring at the Utah mountains, and felt something I hadn't felt in years:

Contentment.

Not survival.

Not scraping by.

Not running on fumes.

Contentment.

I had built more than a cabin.

I had built proof—

proof that I could do hard things,

proof that perseverance mattered,

proof that my story wasn't defined by where I'd started.

From welfare to this.

From homeless shelter to homeowner.

From believing I wasn't educated enough to build a structure—to standing inside one I constructed with my own hands.

The journey was long. Painful. Exhausting.

But standing on that porch, wind in my hair and solid walls behind me, I knew one thing for sure:

I had done it.

And no one could ever take that away from me.

I'd built a cabin with my hands—but God had been building me the whole time.

And now, I finally understood why the journey mattered.

Chapter 27
When Lightning Strikes Twice

The phone rang on a Saturday morning in December 2008.

I was in my temporary housing in South Dakota, enjoying a rare day off from my winter maintenance position at Mount Rushmore. I'd taken the seasonal job specifically because it allowed me to work winters and be home in Utah during summers to finish the cabin.

The cabin was finished now, and I was proud of it. But winter work kept money coming in, and Mount Rushmore was beautiful in its own stark way.

The phone rang again, and I answered without looking at the caller ID.

"Hello?"

"Laurie?" The voice on the other end was shaking. Jason's wife.

My stomach dropped. Something in her tone told me this wasn't a casual call.

"What's wrong?" I asked.

"There's been an accident. It's Jason. He's… he's gone."

The room tilted.

"What?"

She was crying now, words coming in fragments. Winter storm. Kids. Van slid off the road. Jason went to help. Hooking up the van. A car came too fast. Ice. Couldn't stop. Hit his truck.

"He didn't suffer," she said through sobs. "They said it was instant."

Instant.

My funny, caring, responsible son—who always worried about everyone else—was gone.

Just like that.

Helping his family. Doing what Jason always did, showing up when people needed him.

And now he was gone.

I don't remember hanging up the phone. I don't remember getting dressed or grabbing my keys. The next thing I knew, I was driving to the Mount Rushmore work site, desperate to find my coworkers, desperate not to be alone with this news.

They were working that Saturday, and when I burst into the shop, they knew immediately something was wrong.

"My son," I managed to say. "My son is dead."

They surrounded me. Held me while I sobbed. Brought me coffee I couldn't drink. Sat with me in silence when words failed.

I needed to get to Pennsylvania. I needed to see my other kids. I needed to be there for Jason's wife and children, his babies, seven and nine years old, who had just lost their father.

But South Dakota was snowed in.

All roads closed. All flights grounded. The storm that had taken my son now held me captive, unable to leave, unable to do anything but wait.

Saturday passed in a blur of phone calls. Jacob. Heidi. Jason's wife again. My family. Everyone was crying. Everyone was in shock. Everyone asking the same impossible question: How did this happen?

Sunday was worse. The waiting. The helplessness. The reality settled deeper with every hour.

Monday morning, the roads finally opened enough for a flight out.

I flew to Denver, where Jacob and Heidi were waiting. We fell into each other's arms in the airport, three people who had survived so much together, now facing the worst loss of all.

We flew to Pennsylvania together, holding hands during takeoff, trying to be strong for each other and failing.

The funeral was the hardest thing I'd ever endured.

Harder than Steven's death, because I was a child then, too young to fully comprehend loss.

Harder than divorce, homelessness, the welfare lines—because those were challenges, I could fight.

This?

There was no fighting death.

Jason's wife had her life destroyed. His children couldn't understand why Dad wasn't coming home.

The seven-year-old kept asking when he'd wake up.

The nine-year-old stared, silent and hollow.

I wanted to rage. To scream. To demand answers from God about why this kept happening to my family.

Lightning had taken Steven.

Ice had taken Jason.

Both times, they were living their lives.

Both times, they were helping others.

Both times, it was instant, unexpected, unfair.

"Why?" I whispered to God during the service. "Why them? Why my boys?"

No answer came.

Just the weight of grief pressing down on my chest, making it hard to breathe.

I stayed in Pennsylvania a few more days, helping Jason's wife with arrangements, with the kids, with the impossible task of moving forward when your world has shattered.

But I had to go back to South Dakota. I'd taken emergency leave, but I needed to return to work. I needed the structure—needed something to hold onto.

The first week back was mechanical. I showed up. Did my job. Went home. Repeat.

My coworkers were kind—giving me space when I needed it, checking in when I seemed too quiet. But grief is lonely work. No one can do it for you.

So I threw myself into my job.

I worked hard. Took on extra projects. Volunteered for the hardest tasks. If I was working, I wouldn't think. If I wasn't thinking, I wouldn't drown.

By the end of that season at Mount Rushmore, I'd won an award for exceptional performance and dedication.

I stood there accepting it, thinking I'd earned this by running from grief.

But even grief can't be outrun forever.

I worked three seasons at Mount Rushmore after Jason's death.

Three winters of snow and stone.

Three winters of staying busy.

Three winters of telling myself I was fine when I wasn't.

Eventually, I moved on to other parks—different seasons, different landscapes, different challenges. I became a seasonal nomad again, working wherever jobs were available, never staying too long in one place.

Returning to my cabin in Utah between seasons was both comforting and painful.

Jason never had the chance to visit that cabin. I'd worked so hard to create a place for him and his family to come.

Deanna eventually gave up the idea of living there. It was too cold, too hard—chopping firewood all summer just to burn it all winter. She sold her property, moved on, and returned to school full-time in another city.

When I was alone at the cabin, the hardest part was the ladder work—roof repairs, cleaning gutters, anything that required height and trust.

I was terrified of heights. Terrified of one wrong step, one careless moment, one accident that could end everything.

But I'd stand at the bottom of the ladder, hands shaking, and hear Jason's voice in my head:

Come on, Mom. You've got this.

"It's okay," I'd whisper. "Jason's watching me. It's okay."

And I'd climb.

Because that's what we do.

We keep climbing—even when we're scared, even when we're broken, even when we've lost people we can't imagine living without.

We climb anyway.

Jason was my firstborn. My funny kid who could make me laugh even on the worst days. The one who left without warning at nineteen, taking the TV—and my heart—with him.

The one who forgave me for having him sleep in the back of the truck in Colorado. The one who became the glue that held us together.

After the divorce, Jason stepped into a fatherly role—watching out for Jacob and Heidi, checking on me, worrying about all of us in ways a teenage boy should never have had to.

He was responsible. Caring. Protective.

He was my best friend.

And now he was gone.

People say time heals. I don't believe that's true.

Time teaches you how to carry weight without collapsing under it.

Some days were okay. I'd work, laugh with coworkers, enjoy a sunset, feel almost normal.

Other days, I'd see a father with his kids and have to walk away before the tears came.

On the worst days, I'd think about Steven—my little brother, taken by lightning at seven years old—and wonder why loss kept visiting my life.

"Why do You keep taking them?" I'd ask.

But even in my anger, even in my grief, I never stopped believing.

Because faith isn't about understanding God's plan.

It's about trusting Him when the plan makes no sense.

Steven was gone.

Jason was gone.

But I was still here.

And I had to keep going.

For Jacob.

For Heidi.

For Jason's children—who needed to know their grandmother was strong enough to survive this.

For myself.

Years later, I'd be able to think about Jason without crying. I'd tell stories about his humor, his kindness, his love—and smile at the memories instead of drowning in them.

But in those early years, survival was the goal.

One more day.

One more season.

One more climb up that terrifying ladder.

"It's okay," I'd whisper. "Jason's watching."

And I'd believe it.

Because somewhere, somehow, my funny, caring son was still looking out for me—just like he always had.

Even now, when I climb ladders or face something that scares me, I hear his voice:

You've got this, Mom.

And I do.

Not because I'm brave.

Not because I'm strong.

But because Jason taught me that love doesn't end with death.

It transforms—becoming the voice that pushes you forward when you want to quit, the memory that reminds you who you are when grief tries to erase you.

I lost my son in December 2008.

But I didn't lose his love.

And that love—stubborn, protective, always believing I could do more than I thought possible—carried me through the darkest valley I've ever walked.

It still does.

I lost my son that winter, but I didn't lose the part of him that lives in my courage—

and in every step, I take beyond the grief.

Chapter 28
Full Circle-Coming Home

But life has a way of demanding your attention, whether you're ready or not.

Two years after Jason died, Heidi called with news that stopped my heart: cancer. My beautiful, caring daughter—who had already survived so much—was facing a battle that would require intensive treatment. The diagnosis was aggressive, and the treatment plan was no joke.

But here's the thing about Heidi: she doesn't do anything halfway. Not motherhood. Not work. And not fighting cancer.

The chemotherapy was rough—I won't sugarcoat it. But if you think my daughter spent those months lying in bed feeling sorry for herself, you don't know Heidi.

She kept showing up for her two boys.

She kept her sense of humor.

She kept living.

"Some days I feel like I can do this," she admitted once, "and some days I feel like I can't. But I pray, and somehow God gets me through the next hour."

And she meant it.

She beat it the first time with the kind of stubborn determination I recognized—because I'd seen it in the mirror plenty of times myself.

But when the cancer came back a few years later, the doctors recommended something more aggressive: a stem cell transplant.

I didn't fully understand what that meant until Heidi explained it. They would destroy her immune system with high-dose chemotherapy, then rebuild it from donor stem cells. Weeks in the hospital. A month in isolation afterward. Months of recovery.

"How are you doing?" I asked her.

"I'm hanging in there," she said honestly. "But I'm also determined. I have two boys who need their mom—and I've never missed one of their birthdays."

That last part became her battle cry.

Heidi's oldest son had a birthday coming up just weeks after the transplant was scheduled. The doctors told her she'd need to stay in the hospital for at least another month, maybe longer, depending on how her body responded.

"I'll be out before his birthday," Heidi announced.

The doctors were cautious. "We'll see how you do. There are criteria you'll need to meet—"

"Then tell me what they are," she interrupted. "Because I'm meeting them."

And she did.

Every single one.

She worked with the nurses, followed every protocol, pushed herself through the hard days, and stayed focused on one goal: getting home in time for that birthday.

The medical team was amazed. "We've never seen anyone recover this fast," one nurse told her.

Heidi just smiled. "I told you—I don't miss birthdays."

They released her early—not because anyone bent the rules, but because she legitimately met every requirement ahead of schedule.

After the hospital, Heidi had to stay in isolation at a sterile hotel next door while her immune system rebuilt itself. I stayed with her.

We lived in that small room together—me as her only contact with the outside world. I sanitized everything that came in. We cooked simple meals on a hot plate. Played cards. Talked for hours.

But Heidi being Heidi, even isolation couldn't keep her down.

About two weeks in, she looked at me with that mischievous grin I knew meant trouble.

"Mom, I need Mexican food."

I blinked. "Heidi, you're supposed to avoid—"

"I know, I know. No crowds, no exposure, blah blah blah. But Mom, I haven't had real Mexican food in weeks. I'm going crazy."

And she was serious.

"Okay," I said slowly. "How do we do this safely?"

We found a nearby Mexican restaurant. Heidi called ahead and explained the situation. "I just had a stem cell transplant. Can we sit somewhere away from everyone?

The staff was incredible. They seated us in the very back of the restaurant, sanitized the table extra carefully, and treated us like VIPs on a secret mission.

And Heidi? She ordered like she'd been stranded on a desert island.

Enchiladas. Tacos. Rice. Beans. Chips and salsa. The works.

I watched her take that first bite and close her eyes.

"This," she said, grinning, "is what I'm talking about. Cancer can't take this away from me."

We sat in that back corner laughing and eating while she told me stories about the hospital—the nurses she'd befriended, the other patients she'd encouraged, the strange food combinations she'd tried.

Even in the middle of stem cell recovery, with her immune system barely functional, Heidi was still Heidi: spontaneous, funny, determined to live—not just survive.

Some days were harder than others. The isolation wore on her. She missed her boys terribly. There were moments when the reality of what she'd been through would hit, and she'd grow quiet.

But those moments never lasted long.

"God's not done with me yet," she'd say. "I can feel it. He's got plans, and I'm not missing them because I'm sitting around feeling sorry for myself."

After that month, we moved back to her house, though the isolation continued a while longer. Heidi improved quickly, her strength returning day by day.

I stayed with her, helping with the boys. We made healthy smoothies and nutritious meals to rebuild her strength.

She made it home in time to celebrate her son's thirteenth birthday—tired, a little weak, but there. Present. Smiling.

"I'm going to beat this," she told her boys. "And when I do, we're taking road trips. Lots of road trips."

And she did beat it.

The transplant worked. Her immune system rebuilt itself. The isolation ended.

Two-time cancer survivor. My warrior daughter.

Watching Heidi fight cancer twice taught me something powerful: she didn't just survive it. She lived through it.

She found humor in absurd moments. She stayed present for her boys even when exhausted. She encouraged others while healing herself. She snuck out for Mexican food because life is too short not to enjoy the good stuff.

I'd taught her resilience—not through lectures or perfect parenting, but through surviving. Through getting back up. Through refusing to quit.

She's a medical assistant now, caring for others with the same compassion she showed in her own darkest days.

Her two boys are growing into remarkable young men, shaped by a mother who taught them that strength isn't about never falling down.

It's about getting back up—with faith, determination, and maybe a good plate of enchiladas.

That's my Heidi.

Jacob became a master plumber—smart, independent, solving problems the way he always had. He married, has two beautiful children, a boy and a girl, and built a life I'm incredibly proud of.

He's still a Broncos fan. Still the kid who forgave me for dragging him to Colorado all those years ago. We laugh about it now—how angry he was, how he came around, how Colorado shaped him in ways neither of us expected.

My kids survived divorce, poverty, constant moving, and the loss of their brother. They grew into remarkable adults with families of their own.

And somehow, despite everything, we stayed connected.

Life kept shifting.

Deanna moved on, found new opportunities, and became a licensed nurse.

Mom moved back to Utah in her late seventies. I returned to my cabin, took local Park Service work, and became her caretaker.

For four years, I cared for my mother.

The woman who'd been absent for much of my childhood now needed me daily. We never became warm or affectionate, but we found something else: companionship, mutual respect, peace.

I cooked her meals, arranged Meals on Wheels, drove her to appointments, managed medications, and checked on her every day.

It wasn't easy. Old wounds don't disappear just because someone needs help. But I showed up anyway.

When she passed away at eighty-two, I felt relief mixed with grief. Relief that she was no longer suffering. Grief for the relationship we never fully had.

But we'd made peace. And that was enough.

After Mom died, I was alone in Utah.

The cabin was beautiful, everything I'd dreamed of—but living there year-round, alone, in a tight-knit community where I'd always been an outsider, was harder than I expected.

The winters were brutal. Isolating.

Life revolved around one rhythm: chop wood, carry wood, stack wood, burn wood. Repeat.

It was exhausting. And lonely.

My kids were scattered. I was proud of them—but I was the only one left tending fires and scraping ice, wondering if this was really where I wanted to stay.

I loved that cabin. Every board represented something I'd overcome.

But it was time to let go.

In 2019, I put the cabin on the market.

It sold for a good price, enough to give me options.

I packed up my life one more time. Not running. Not escaping.

Choosing.

I moved to southern Arizona—Hereford, to be exact—where winter means sixty degrees and sunshine, not survival.

I bought a small place. Nothing fancy. But it's mine.

I retired in 2024.

Officially. Finally.

From welfare lines to national parks.

From homeless shelters to a home, I built myself.

From a terrified single mother to a woman who raised three remarkable children.

One I lost too soon.

All of whom I'm proud of.

Looking back, I see God's hand everywhere.

In the jobs that came at exactly the right time.

In the people who showed up when I needed them most.

In the strength I found when I thought I had nothing left.

Faith wasn't always easy. There were years I was angry at God, questioning why He kept taking people I loved.

But He never left.

Every hard season prepared me for what came next.

Now, sitting in my Arizona home, watching the sun set over mountains I don't have to climb anymore, I can see it clearly.

All of it was building toward this.

A life of peace.

Of contentment.

Of knowing I survived—and thrived.

If you're reading this and you feel trapped—by poverty, fear, or circumstances, I want you to know something:

You can get out.

It won't be easy. But keep going. One step at a time.

Ask for help. Use what you have. Believe your story still matters.

Because it does.

Break the boundaries that tell you you're not good enough, strong enough, or worthy enough.

You are.

You always have been.

And your story isn't over yet.

The best chapters are still waiting—just beyond the boundaries you dare to break.

In Memory of

Steven Robert Cowen (1958-1965)
Jason Rienhardt Spencer (1978–2008)
Louise Adelaide Narvick (1934–2017)

About the Author

Laurie E. Spencer has spent a lifetime exploring the landscapes of both the natural world and the human spirit. From the challenges of growing up on welfare to the breathtaking peaks of Yellowstone, Laurie's journey is a testament to resilience, faith, and the courage to pursue a life of purpose and adventure.

A storyteller at heart, Laurie blends vivid memories from her own life with thoughtful reflections, inviting readers to walk beside her through moments of struggle, discovery, and triumph. In addition to her memoirs, she writes Bible study books that inspire, encourage, and bring humor and insight to readers seeking to grow in their faith.

Laurie lives in Hereford, Arizona, where she continues to write, hike, and encourage others to embrace their own journeys with courage, determination, and faith.

+

Also, by Laurie E. Spencer

Books and Bible Studies

To the Gallows and Beyond

Chuckling Through God's Word: A Bible Study

Holy Giggles: A 12-Part Bible Study

Holy Humor: A 12-Part Bible Study

The Sing King: From Shepherd Boy to King – A Bible Study

Breaking Boundaries: Parts One and Two – Bible Studies

📖 Get your copies today and start breaking boundaries!

Visit: www.holygiggles.com

Made in the USA
Coppell, TX
22 February 2026

72091782R00138